BFI FILM

....

Rob ✔ **KU-517-177**

S E R I E S   E D I T O R

Edward Buscombe, Colin MacCabe and David Meeker

S E R I E S   C O N S U L T A N T S

Cinema is a fragile medium. Many of the great films now exist, if at all, in damaged or incomplete prints. Concerned about the deterioration in the physical state of our film heritage, the National Film and Television Archive, part of the British Film Institute's Collections Department, has compiled a list of 360 key works in the history of the cinema. The long-term goal of the Archive is to build a collection of perfect showprints of these films, which will then be screened regularly at the National Film Theatre in London in a year-round repertory.

BFI Film Classics is a series of books intended to introduce, inter-pret and honour these 360 films. Critics, scholars, novelists and those distinguished in the arts have been invited to write on a film of their choice, drawn from the Archive's list. The numerous illustrations have been made specially from the Archive's own prints.

With new titles published each year, the BFI Film Classics series is a unique, authoritative and highly readable guide to the masterpieces of world cinema.

The best movie publishing idea of the [past] decade.
Philip French, *The Observer*

A remarkable series which does all kinds of varied and divergent things.
Michael Wood, *Sight and Sound*

Exquisitely dimensioned ... magnificently concentrated examples of freeform critical poetry.
Uncut

Resnais on set

BFI FILM

CLASSICS

L'ANNÉE DERNIÈRE
À MARIENBAD

. . . .

Jean-Louis Leutrat

TRANSLATED BY PAUL HAMMOND

 Publishing

First published in 2000 by the
BRITISH FILM INSTITUTE
21 Stephen Street, London W1P 2LN

The British Film Institute
promotes greater understanding
and appreciation of, and
access to, film and moving image
culture in the UK.

British Library Cataloguing-in-Publication Data
A catalogue record for this book is available from the British Library

ISBN 0–85170–821–8

Series design by
Andrew Barron & Collis Clements Associates

Typeset in Fournier and Franklin Gothic by
D R Bungay Associates, Burghfield, Berks

CONTENTS

. . . .

1

A Controversial Work *7*

2

The Film's Background *10*

3

The Genesis of the Film *17*

4

A Description of the Film *28*

5

The Two 'L'Année dernière à Marienbad' *52*

6

'L'Année dernière à Marienbad' and the
History of Cinema *62*

Notes *68*

Credits *70*

Bibliography *71*

in memory of my father

Resnais with Delphine Seyrig

1
. . . .
A CONTROVERSIAL WORK

At the time of its release *L'Année dernière à Marienbad* had its fierce
critics as well as its staunch supporters. Among the former was Michel
Mourlet: 'No notion of acting, no grasp of the rudiments of décor, no
feeling for narrative, nothing but pathetic little intellectual games which
solemnly play at being cinema.'[1] Years later this text would echo in
Jacques Lourcelles's dictionary entry, where it states that Resnais's film,
'one of the most insane the cinema has ever produced', is not of 'notable'
interest, which is tantamount to saying that it has none.[2]

In the other camp, Jacques Brunius wrote in 1962 in *Sight and
Sound* that *L'Année dernière à Marienbad* was 'the film I had been waiting
for during the last thirty years', adding: 'I am now quite prepared to claim
that *Marienbad* is the greatest film ever made, and to pity those who
cannot see this.'[3] In 1963 the magazine *Artsept* published a collection of
writings on the film, which opened with an extract from the letter an
'incredibly moved and dazzled' Michel Leiris had written to Alain
Resnais on 20 May 1961:

> Subdued by the images and imbued by all the words he hears, the
> viewer willingly enters into the film (or allows himself to be
> penetrated by it!) and finds himself transfixed by an endless stream of
> prodigious tableaux akin (in their eternal fixity of purpose and their
> power of fascination) to those that memories and desires can offer him
> at the most intense moments of his daily life – something very close,
> in short, to what Sartre describes as 'privileged situations'.[4]

Philosophers in particular were instantly enamoured of Resnais's
film. In 1963 Geneviève Rodis-Lewis, an expert on Descartes and
Malebranche, published a text called 'Mirror of My Thought' which ends
with a superlative analysis of the long 'bleached-out' tracking shot:

> An absolutely cinematic language is elaborated here which reaches
> the intellect only when it has first passed through the senses, as the
> philosophers would say. This is the paroxysm of desire, the vertigo
> of *amour fou*, an invention particular to Resnais, rather than the

unacceptable fantasy of rape described in the screenplay. ... Is this not, indeed, the blinding spark which ultimately links the poles X and A?[5]

In 1968 Gilles Deleuze alluded in *Différence et répétition* to Resnais's film as 'bearing witness to the particular techniques of repetition which the cinema employs, or invents'.[6] Fifteen years later this analysis was extended and widened in the already classic pages of *L'Image-temps* devoted to '*undecidable alternatives* between layers of the past'.[7]

If Resnais's film has today entered history it is still by no means a familiar work. Furthermore, traces remain of the old rivalries between cinema lovers of a generation which, with every passing day, becomes more distanced in time: these rivalries are a sign of the passions cinema excited, of the immaturity of certain 'commentators', and the blindness which can strike spectators otherwise endowed with sensibility.

The names in the *L'Année dernière à Marienbad* credits are presented in relief letters on a grey background, as on certain visiting or invitation cards. We are being summoned to a ceremony, or to a soirée: the characters are dressed accordingly, they will express themselves in rather formal language; we are invited to adopt this posture in advance, 'out of pure convention'. There are works created which lean towards the formal, and some may find them boring and academic.

Roughly speaking, there are two kinds of film-maker: Eisenstein or Sternberg on the one hand, Rossellini or Cassavetes on the other. Apropos of Alain Resnais's film Claude Ollier wrote:

> As to the interdictions pronounced in the name of 'naturalness' and 'spontaneity', they have absolutely no meaning. The only thing that counts is the rigour (hence the strength of conviction, hence the truth) with which the materials are organised, whatever their origin and the degree of artifice binding them together. ... It is by pushing the 'artificial' to the extreme that Alain Resnais and Alain Robbe-Grillet have managed to create an exemplarily true work.[8]

Added to which, humour is not absent from Resnais's film. The person who perhaps best defined the effect this film was capable of producing (and which it perhaps still produces) is Robert Benayoun, when he wrote:

'Slipperily hieratic, coldly dishevelled, starchily fluid, playfully lugubrious, casually deliberate, glacially frenetic', adding:

> This work-shy work, at once constructed and deconstructed, in which all was meticulously foreseen save the essential, namely the breeze that whisks it away, the grace that suffuses it, the inestimable and timeless charm it exudes, this work of which we mainly retain the frame, whatever we might do with this, one of the high points of the imaginary of our time, largely lives through the presence of the beings who populate it: they cast a shadow in places (those famous yews lopped into pyramids) where no shadow is cast.[9]

For the novelist Jean-Louis Bory *L'Année dernière à Marienbad* was a disturbing, obsessive and difficult film.[10] Disturbing because it repeatedly calls psychological realism, and its corollaries causality and linearity, into question. Obsessive because it's necessary to see it many times and to allow one's admiration to gradually give way to emotion. Difficult because it requires the spectator to make an effort to engage with it. Obsessive, it surely is. Difficult depends on the viewer. As for disturbing, the word seems excessive: if we grant to a film the possibility of having a poetic rather than traditionally fictional ambition, if we do not take the cinema to be a mechanism meant exclusively for telling stories, if we accept that a work might surprise us and propose something different to what we're accustomed to, then this film is no more disturbing than it is obscure, something it has often been reproached for being. In *L'Année dernière à Marienbad* a game is made of the rules. There are pieces on a checker or chessboard, some cards, with a traditional Western setting: a chateau and a garden. The film's deviations are as complex as those of the human heart. *L'Année dernière à Marienbad* demands that it be submitted to the 'reasons' of the heart.

2

. . . .

THE FILM'S BACKGROUND

Alain Resnais

Born on 3 June 1922 in the Brittany town of Vannes, Alain Resnais was the only child of an average middle-class family. His father was a pharmacist. He went to a religious school: 'I had a very strict Catholic upbringing in Brittany,' he has said, 'and I hate thinking back to my childhood.' Subject to attacks of asthma, he was of delicate health. His mother encouraged his education and would seem to have given him a taste for classical music. His parents had a property in the Golfe du Morbihan. He was to recall this landscape in *Mon Oncle d'Amérique*:

> The island you see in the bay is in the Golfe du Morbihan. It's one of the four hundred islands in the bay, and legend has it that there are as many of them as there are days in the year. I used to go there as a kid, keeping it a secret from my family. Secretly, because I wasn't allowed to go sailing on the open sea, I was 8 or 10 at the time and I'd wait until my family went off before getting the dinghy out. I never saw my grandfather roasting crabs but I used to roast them myself. I adored that. My friends and I used to lark about on the sand and we even tried putting sand on the fire because the Egyptians had discovered glass that way. We never managed it though.

In 1940 he left for the Midi, with the intention of reaching Algeria. He remained in Nice, where he prepared his baccalaureate. He would evoke this period in *L'Amour à mort*: 'I can remember seeing shepherds and their flocks on the Riviera at Nice.'

In 1941 he arrived in Paris, where his asthma instantly disappeared. In 1943 the French cinema school, the IDHEC, was set up and an editor friend, Myriam, advised him to enrol. He passed the entrance exam, coming second. He thus formed part of the first intake of students, enrolling as an editor; Henri Colpi was a co-student. He took up 14 x 10 photography, specialising in portraiture. Disappointed by the teaching, apart from one lecture by Jean Grémillon, he resigned a year later. In 1946 he made three 16mm films with Gérard Philipe (they lived in the same Rue du Dragon building) and Danielle Delorme. A dozen visits with painters followed in 1947. Myriam, the film editor, got him a job cutting *Le Roman d'un tricheur*. He was assistant editor in 1947 on Nicole Vedrès's *Paris 1900*, and subsequently editor on many films between 1952–8. Pierre Braunberger suggested he make a series of shorts. This would include *Van Gogh* in 1948, then *Paul Gauguin* and *Guernica* in 1950.

His output grew during the 50s. Short films in the first instance, some of which, like *Nuit et brouillard* (1955) and *Toute la mémoire du monde* (1956), brought him renown. *Hiroshima mon amour* (1959) was his first feature. The latter part of the 60s marked a change in his style. *La Guerre est finie* in 1966 appeared to deviate from his earlier 'experimental' work. In 1967 he directed a sequence in *Loin de Vietnam* and in 1968, at the request of Chris Marker, he filmed a cine-tract. May '68 saw the release of *Je t'aime, je t'aime*, which was a commercial failure. Resnais received no more offers and left for New York, where he remained from 1969 (the year he married Florence Malraux) to 1971, working on a number of projects which came to nothing, notably with the comics creator Stan Lee (*The Monster Maker*, 1970; *The Inmates*, 1971). He also proposed *Conan* to a producer, without success. His career took off again in 1974 with *Biarritz-Bonheur* (or *Stavisky*), a work that was badly received by the critics, but which proved a success with the public.

Alain Robbe-Grillet

Like Resnais, Alain Robbe-Grillet is Breton in origin; like him he was born in 1922, on 18 August, in Brest. He received his secondary and higher education in Paris. He became an agronomist and worked at the National Statistics Institute, afterwards doing laboratory research in biology. In 1950–1 he was an engineer at the Institute of Tropical and Citrus Fruits. He was sent on missions to Morocco, Guinea, Martinique and Guadeloupe. He published his first novel, *Les Gommes*, in 1953. Two years later he became a literary adviser at Éditions de Minuit. That same year he published his first articles and his second novel, *Le Voyeur*, which was awarded the Critics' Prize. *Dans le labyrinthe* (1959) was his third novel. In 1961 he worked on *L'Année dernière à Marienbad*, of which he was the script and dialogue writer. Two years later he made his first film, *L'Immortelle*, and published *Pour un nouveau roman*. Since then he has had a career as writer, film-maker and lecturer.

Structuralism and the 'Nouveau Roman'

Claude Lévi-Strauss, and the first volume of his *Anthroplogie structurale*, announced the arrival of structuralism; in January 1959 a colloquium was organised around the word 'structure'. Roland Barthes proposed a new approach to 'classical' writers (Michelet, for example, and then Racine). In the literary field at the beginning of the 60s, and according to the principle of the overlapping of the generations, authors like Louis Aragon, Raymond Queneau and Jean-Paul Sartre occupied pride of place, while the representatives of the 'New Novel' began producing their first works: Michel Butor (*La Modification*, 1957), Alain Robbe-Grillet (*La Jalousie*, 1957), Nathalie Sarraute (*L'Ere du soupçon*, 1956), Jean Cayrol (*Le Vent de la mémoire*, 1951), Marguerite Duras (*Moderato Cantabile*, 1958), Claude Simon (*Le Vent*, 1957), Robert Pinget (*Graal Filibuste*, 1957), and Robbe-Grillet published his programmatic statement 'A Way Ahead for the Novel of the Future'.

As it is, the name of Robbe-Grillet is linked to the *nouveau roman*, a term designating a literary movement having no leader, review or manifesto, and which lumps a certain number of writers together. Considered a 'school of the gaze', of the 'objective' – or worse still, 'objectual' – novel, the *nouveau roman* is in appearance abstract, formalist and difficult to read. In fact, it proposed a renewal of narration by contesting the idea of 'literariness', that is, the psychological construction of a character, a linear story, the identity of beings, things and places. Roland Barthes praised what for him was the new writer's main contribution from 1954 onward: 'Robbe-Grillet's ambition is to found the novel of surface.' The novels of Robbe-Grillet present a world without quality, without meaning, out of the need to escape all morality or metaphysics, as well as all psychology. From his first novel on his technique was considered to be that of cold description. Images proliferate, are imbricated with each other to the point where precise events become diluted in each of our consciousnesses, leaving only uncertainty.

It has been said that the closed world of Robbe-Grillet's novels refers to the collapse of a certain rationalist ideal, and that the place accorded to the aleatory in such work 'is an indictment of bourgeois determinism'. The ideological crisis of Communism began with the 20th Congress. It was clear that a turning point was being reached which would inevitably lead to a serious readjustment of ideas. In France in

1958 General de Gaulle exercised the power he'd obtained as President of the Republic. Coming immediately after the war in Indo-China, the Algerian conflict weighed heavily in the political balance of the time. Economically, France acceded to mass consumerism. Family incomes went on rising. The new franc was created; the Common Market came into being. There was nothing to either confirm or to deny assertions establishing a mechanistic relation between works of art and the politico-economic context of their elaboration, yet such assertions do not allow us to get very far in understanding these works.

Such an approach has obviously been tried in relation to *L'Année dernière à Marienbad*. At the time of its release – and this is still true today – the film appeared, in effect, as an expression of the critique of 'literariness' to which the *nouveau roman* bore witness. The school of the gaze, the absence of man, the bias towards things and objects, are positions which, it might be thought, belonged to Resnais as well, especially since at the end of the 50s and early 60s the film-maker worked with writers associated with the *nouveau roman*. *L'Année dernière à Marienbad* has also been likened to Luis Buñuel's *Exterminating Angel* (1962), owing to the theme of confinement in a single place – the confinement, of course, of a social class.

The Renewal of Cinema
The 50s were of great richness where cinema is concerned. They were also marked in France by the development of film criticism, notably through magazines like *Cahiers du Cinéma*, *Positif*, *Cinéma*, *Image et Son*, and the weekly columns published in *Les Lettres françaises*, *Arts*, etc. In 1958 André Bazin, critic on *Cahiers du Cinéma*, of which he was to some degree the main theorist, died. His development of criticism accustomed a certain kind of viewer to a more intellectual approach towards films; it also led to greater reflection on cinema and its reciprocal relation with the other arts.

In 1958–9 many directors created works of vital importance: Michelangelo Antonioni (*Il Grido*), Ingmar Bergman (*Wild Strawberries*), Luchino Visconti (*White Nights*), Alfred Hitchcock (*Vertigo*), Orson Welles (*Touch of Evil*), Anthony Mann (*Man of the West*), Howard Hawks (*Rio Bravo*). Other major works, such as Kenji Mizoguchi's *Ugetsu Monogotari* (1953), were seen in the West for the first time. Hollywood classicism entered its terminal phase. In Europe and in other countries new forms were appearing. A transformation was at work which attempted to address the fact that the situation, the viewpoint one could have of the world, had changed. The cinema was obliged to communicate this idea of complexity while taking care, as far as Resnais was concerned at least, to address itself to the viewer 'in a *critical way*. To achieve this [he] tries to make films which aren't natural. Realistic cinema, the reconstitution of everyday life, the reproduction of gestures, is something [he] doesn't find interesting.'[11]

Although in France the cinema represented by René Clair, Marcel Carné, Julien Duvivier, Claude Autant-Lara and Christian-Jaque had entered into decline, some of the works that would commend themselves to the so-called New Wave directors were just then appearing: *Une Vie* (Alexandre Astruc), *Mon Oncle* (Jacques Tati), *Deux Hommes dans Manhattan* (Jean-Pierre Melville), *Pickpocket* (Robert Bresson). Getting their chance to direct were Louis Malle (*Les Amants* and *Ascenseur pour l'échafaud*), Georges Franju (*La Tête contre les murs*), Jean Rouch (*Moi, un Noir*) and François Truffaut (*Les 400 Coups*). New directors were also emerging abroad (in America Arthur Penn with *The Lefthanded Gun*; in England 'Free Cinema' film-makers Tony Richardson, Lindsay Anderson, Karel Reisz); barely known national cinemas were being discovered (the Polish, for instance, with Andrzej Wajda and *Kanal*), while Hammer 'horror' films made their appearance in Great Britain with Terence Fisher's *Dracula*. The 50s also witnessed the European breakthrough of Japanese cinema with two works by Akira Kurosawa: *Rashomon* in 1952 and *The Seven Samurai* in 1955. The Palme d'or at the 1954 Cannes Film Festival went to Teinsuke Kinugasa's *Gates of Hell*.

Resnais's tastes were in things cinematic. From 1958–61 – the period between *Hiroshima mon amour* and *L'Année dernière à Marienbad* – he actually gave a list to *Cahiers du Cinéma*, in no order of preference, of the ten best films for each of these years. This list bears witness to an extremely varied taste which extends from Karel Zeman's animation film *Fantastic Adventures* to Bert Stern's documentary *Jazz on a Summer's Day*; his love of musical comedy shows through in his choice of Stanley Donen and George Abbot's *The Pajama Game* and Joshua Logan's *South Pacific* (no doubt because this was a remake of a famous Broadway show by Rodgers and Hammerstein), and he includes two films on the concentration camps in his list (Konrad Wolf's *Sterne* and Armand Gatti's *L'Enclos*). Listed are the new French film-makers Godard, Malle,

Kast, Rouch, Rivette, Truffaut, Colpi, Marker, Astruc, and a few older ones (Bresson, Cocteau). Even if account is taken of the sympathies linking Resnais to some of these film-makers, the names listed will endure. The same is true for the foreign directors, with Antonioni, Mizoguchi, Bergman, Wajda, Satyajit Ray, Cassavetes, Hawks, Welles, Lang, Hitchcock. Resnais gave his views on some of these film-makers (to mention only the Italians): of Michelangelo Antonioni, 'At a certain level I actually believe our preoccupations overlap'; and of Luchino Visconti, 'Do I like him? It's more than that! Have you seen *White Nights* in the original Italian version? ... He extracts a rare charm from language. I saw the film six times.'

Resnais's relationship with the cinema began very early on. Vannes had two cinemas, but he was only allowed into the local one, where he enthused over *Robin Hood* and Julien Duvivier's *Mystère de la tour Eiffel* (both 1923). At nine he saw Jean Epstein's *Mor Vran* (1931) and *Or des mers* (1932). His cousin also showed him films on a Pathé-Baby projector: a documentary, an animated cartoon and a Harold Lloyd (*Haunted Spooks*, 1920), plus Abel Gance's *Napoleon* (1926). In 1936 Resnais shot a version of *Fantômas* on 8mm, using local kids from Vannes as the actors, converting a small room into a cinema. He showed Charlie Chase and Laurel and Hardy films there each week, and every two months a feature. 'I started practising that technique [accompanying the projection of a silent film with music] when I was eleven or twelve; I used to put on film shows for my friends at eleven on a Thursday morning, with movies from the Cinémathèque Kodak, and I'd play gramophone records.'

In 1936 Resnais continued his education in Paris, lodging with a priest who took in boarders. Thursdays and Sundays he went to the cinema: 'I remember that after seeing John Ford's *The Informer* I displayed such enthusiasm in front of this priest that he gave me the nickname "Simple Alain".' In 1942 Resnais worked as an extra on *Les Visiteurs du soir*. He frequented the by now legendary cinemas Studio 28 and Les Ursulines (with presentations by Langlois, who 'never managed to finish a sentence'). At the Cinémathèque he discovered Feuillade in 1939, and again in 1944, plus the writings of Jean Epstein, such as *Bonjour cinéma*. *La Règle du jeu* (1939) was a revelation:

On coming out of the cinema I plonked myself down on the edge of the pavement and sat rigid for a good five minutes, then I found myself walking the streets of Paris for a couple of hours. Everything was topsy-turvy, all my ideas about cinema had been turned upside-down. My impressions were so strong during the projection that if certain sequences had been longer by as much as a shot they'd have reduced me to tears or to hysterics.

Other favourites included Cocteau's *Le Sang d'un poète* (1930) and the films of Sacha Guitry.

The desire to go into directing was to grow out of this fertile environment:

I'd been present as a youngster at a performance of *Ceux de chez nous* at the Théâtre de la Madeleine, and Sacha Guitry had shown us clips from the films he'd made on painters like Renoir, Monet and Degas and on other famous people like Sarah Bernhardt. I said to myself that maybe it would be amusing to show painters when they're young and not in their dotage.

3

. . . .

THE GENESIS OF THE FILM

The Resnais/Robbe-Grillet collaboration

By 1961 Resnais was accustomed to working with writers. He'd been struck, in 1943, by the beauty of the language in Robert Bresson's *Les Anges du péché*: 'Someone had finally asked Giraudoux to write a script.' Two years later the 'intense musicality' of Cocteau's dialogue for *Les Dames du Bois de Boulogne* delighted him. After collaborating with Raymond Queneau and Paul Éluard, Resnais joined forces with Jean Cayrol, Marguerite Duras and finally Alain Robbe-Grillet. In 1965 Claude Simon crossed swords with Eric Rohmer during a lively debate; he used Resnais's work to argue that 'modern cinema could not exist were it not for the subjective image, that is, unless the image was a mental image, as it is in Resnais.' This echoed a remark made by Robbe-Grillet in 1963 about the attraction cinematic creation had for the New Novelists:

> It isn't the objectivity of the camera that enthuses them, but its possibilities in the domain of the subjective, of the imaginary. They don't conceive of cinema as a means of expression, but of research, and what most claims their attention is, naturally, what was most lacking in the means of literature: namely, not so much the image but the soundtrack – the sound of voices, different noises, atmospheres, kinds of music – and above all the possibility of acting on two senses at once, the eye and the ear.[12]

In June 1959 *Hiroshima mon amour* was presented to the public; during winter 1959–60 two producers, Pierre Courau and Raymond Froment, arranged a meeting between Alain Resnais and Alain Robbe-Grillet. The director hadn't read any of the novelist's books, and he made up for lost time. As for Robbe-Grillet, he was preparing to shoot a film, a project he would set aside to work with Resnais. The two men spoke at length and were to 'come to an understanding on the notion of exploring non-narrative "cinematic forms" based on a certain *indecipherable* quality'.[13] In an interview Robbe-Grillet said:

We began by speaking of things like glances that are directed off-screen, what linkages are needed when relations of causality are altogether uncertain, ambiguity, the obscure nature of the slightest amorous adventure. And we found that we were agreed on all that. The question of defining an anecdote was something for later: the important thing was in the telling. As long as the kinds of form were agreed on, we'd be able to think up the subject.[14]

Robbe-Grillet proposed four subjects, *L'Immortelle* (a project he'd already completed), a story taking place in a cinema studio, another one in the countryside, and a project entitled *L'Année dernière* (the 'Marienbad' would come later). A series of discussions followed aimed at making a choice. 'We chose the one I found the most sentimental and austere,' the director has said. Next, Robbe-Grillet handed in a weekly instalment, until the task was complete. The whole thing was presented as an image-by-image description, with dialogue and indications about camera movements and sound. This work over, the two men discussed it at length (eight days of talks) and reached total agreement, as they stated to the press. They then went their separate ways, Robbe-Grillet leaving for Brest, then Turkey, with Resnais preparing and directing the film.

With Robbe-Grillet in Istanbul, Resnais said they had 'a friendly correspondence which I barely recall. I asked him to modify four or five replies out of the craftsman-like wish of being more fully understood by the public. He took pleasure in copying them out for me in his magnificent handwriting.'[15] It's interesting to note here that Resnais claimed to remember only the handwriting of Robbe-Grillet. We will return to this at the end of the chapter.

When Robbe-Grillet, now back from Turkey, saw the film he discovered that Resnais had added 'a bit of psychology'. Resnais recalled:

He didn't take me to task because he found it 'very beautiful, in a word', but he merrily and good-humouredly added that on that score I'd betrayed him. What he also questioned, while recognising its effectiveness for the public, was the music. He found it too sugary, too limp, too sentimental. He'd have liked something aggressive, more strident. On top of that, I think he'd imagined other actors.[16]

Made much of at the time of the film's release, the agreement between the two men was to all intents and purposes a mere façade. Their highly orchestrated 'disagreement' came out when it came to replying to a more minor question; on the fact, for instance, that the characters had or hadn't met in a problematic past: probably not, according to the novelist, the film-maker's response being the opposite. At the same time this artful little game set the wheel of interpretation turning, and this became all the rage after the release of the film, which became a riddle, a parlour game.

Convergences, divergences

In 1956 Resnais made a short, *Toute la mémoire du monde*, which already predicted the common ground shared by the film-maker and Robbe-Grillet. It was a 'documentary' on the Bibliothèque Nationale. The chief cameraman on the film, Ghislain Cloquet, was to say: 'Before Resnais made Marienbad you'd have been hard put to realise that here was a mental space. In *Toute la mémoire* Resnais unquestionably created a rough draft of what was to become one of his greatest films.'[17] That architecture can be the image of a psychic state is nothing new in cinema. One could cite numerous examples of architecture or architectural details being 'symbolically' called on to represent the mental state of an individual or a group of people: the spiral staircase in *Vertigo* (1958), the house in *Psycho* (1960) and in *Gaslight* (1940, 1944), the city in *Metropolis* (1925) and most of the edifices in 'fantastic' cinema (the Dracula-style castles or Count Zaroff's fortress). Yet it is by no means certain that Resnais sought to

Toute la mémoire du monde

describe the mental state of a particular individual, or even of a group of people. The Bibliothèque Nationale is, first and foremost, a mental space: it doesn't facilitate a return to the past; it is, rather, the image of a collective future already inscribed in the present. The comparisons which go to form the description of the Bibliothèque (prison, hospital) are all prescient variations on what Foucault has called 'the Great Confinement'. Confinement does not refer to the turning back on itself of consciousness, but to an endeavour in which the whole human race is trapped inside an immense, labyrinthine laboratory. This theme of the labyrinth is also found in Robbe-Grillet, who published *Dans le labyrinthe* in 1959.

It is quite possible, what's more, to discover further parallels between Robbe-Grillet's world and that of *L'Année dernière à Marienbad* – it would be astonishing were this not so. In *La Jalousie* a young woman (A) is the central character around whom hover Franck, her potential lover, and an invisible narrator, a fanatical observer, probably her husband. The situation is not without echoes of the film, in the 'scenario' of which the young woman is designated by the same letter; added to which the arrival, or the presence 'last year', of someone called Franck is repeatedly announced by the occupants of the hotel. Nevertheless, the fact should not be ignored that Resnais has literary tastes which have led him in a direction other than that of the *nouveau roman*. At the age of fourteen he discovered Cocteau's *Le Potomac*, then the Surrealists, Philippe Soupault's *Le Bon Apôtre*, and afterwards *Le Paysan de Paris*, *Nadja* and the *Manifestoes of Surrealism*. As a child his sensibility also developed in a climate conducive to the supernatural. One of his childhood readings was *La Légende de la mort chez les Bretons armoricains* [*The Legend of Death Among the Armorican Bretons*] by Anatole Le Braz.

His grandmother's sister was famous for having seen from her window the funeral procession of a woman neighbour who was considered to be in perfect health and whose death had been unannounced; the latter was to occur eight days later, with the procession passing exactly as the prophetess had seen it, thanks to a leap-forward in time. The strange adventure that had befallen his grandfather's uncle was often recounted to the young Alain. The man had come across a ghostly figure inscribing a particular latitude and longitude in the log of the ship he captained. This gave the position of a vessel that was sinking. At the prow of the first lifeboat returning with the survivors stood the ghost.

It could be argued that the film is closest to a literary tradition to which a writer faithful to André Breton and Surrealism, to Julien Gracq (who has written some extremely harsh things about Robbe-Grillet's work), or, going further back in time, to a 'Romantic' like Gérard de Nerval belongs. We read, in Gracq's *Le Rivage des Syrtes*: 'I proceeded to slowly move from room to room, while casting a bored glance at the frozen saraband of the ceilings and frescoes, like some museum visitor.' We recognise the slow tracking shot at the beginning of the film; we may also recall the young woman in *L'Année dernière à Marienbad* thanks the man who has just been describing the ornamental detail on the hotel walls to her with the words: 'I'd never had such a good guide before.' In one of Nerval's narratives, *Sylvie*, we never know what time-frame we're in: the beloved is now a peasant girl, now an actress, now a young noblewoman who has withdrawn to a convent, etc. Each evening the suitor is present, like a spectator in the theatre, at a magical ritual of regeneration. We may ask ourselves if the spectacle to which we're invited by the opening of *L'Année dernière à Marienbad* does not play just such a regenerative role.

Resnais manifests a love of theatre unknown in Robbe-Grillet. During his childhood the theatre in Vannes offered him only the most mediocre of entertainments:

> [it] was so much in ruins that people used to sit on garden chairs, and they took the precaution of bringing blankets and umbrellas because, in the event of a downpour, the rain came right through the auditorium roof. The entrance was very strange. In the tiny street there were two absolutely identical porches with nothing to tell them apart. One led to the theatre and the other to the Gents.

On the other hand, when he used to visit Paris at Christmas and Easter with his grandfather he saw a number of plays that captivated him: *La Guerre de Troie n'aura pas lieu*, with Louis Jouvet; *Le Faiseur*, with Charles Dullin; *La Fin du monde*, with Sacha Guitry; Henri Bernstein's *Espoir*, with Claude Dauphin; and especially Pitoëff in *La Mouette* at the Mathurins in 1937, which triggered an undying passion in him for the theatre.

Other differences exist between Resnais and Robbe-Grillet. Resnais is interested in comic strips and popular novels (he has never made any secret of his passion for Jean Ray's *Les Aventures de Harry Dickson*), while Robbe-Grillet is more attracted to the photo-novel and magazine images. The obsessive return, in both his films and his novels, to the stereotyped eroticism transmitted by these magazines is absolutely alien to Resnais. However, it mustn't be forgotten that the *nouveau roman* has two 'currents': one that may be called descriptive or scientific, resulting in the impersonal vision of a universe reduced to a sum of 'objects'; and the other 'subjectivist', leading to a more oneiric or symbolic literature. Convergences and divergences are the order of things, then; they constitute one aspect of the film which deserves particular attention, because in it a major moment within European culture is subtly in play.

The Filming

Resnais's different collaborators have been unusually forthcoming. We can, then, retrace the various stages of the film and even try and imagine what it might have become if Resnais had had greater means at his disposal: 'I've never made such a difficult film. Resnais is the first to find the film a bit slap-dash. And I agree with him.'[18]

The anecdotes can be set alongside each other. For instance, the connection between one of the characters mentioning the water in the ornamental ponds which had frozen over 'last year' and the cold weather that occurred during shooting: 'Imagine what it means to film in an evening dress in those freezing rooms.'[19] The set designer Jacques Saulnier also tells us that 'the Marienbad set was in colours. ... The walls were pink and the mouldings silver. This pink tone was extremely odd, but it photographed beautifully, a beautiful grey.'[20]

Saulnier was taken on four months before shooting. He had a conversation at that time with Robbe-Grillet 'who didn't give much away'. The location where the film was to be shot was the subject of some

Resnais directing Giorgio Albertazzi and Seyrig

hesitation: Aix-les-Bains, perhaps? The novelist had the Cercle interallié in mind. Why not? The India of Duras's *India Song* (1975) would be suggested by such anachronisms. 'To begin with everything was to be arranged in Paris, and I remember visiting the Hôtel d'Orsay, at the far end of the Gare d'Orsay, because Kast, who often stayed there, had told us it had a corridor 150 metres long, and that we absolutely had to see it. It was a bit of a lie, there was practically nothing left of it.'[21] Finally the locations would be on the outskirts of Munich: Nymphenburg, Amalienburg, Schleissheim, the Munich Antiquarium.

Some of the anecdotes are, of course, about technical problems. According to the lighting cameraman Sacha Vierny the first few days were extremely hard. The film was in 'Scope. According to Jean Léon the use made of this was 'astonishing'.[22] Philippe Brun, the camera operator, has described how 'We shot, then, in 50mm 'Scope, which is the lens normally used when there's movement.'[23] And Sacha Vierny:

> While the 'Scope format usually implies a certain immobility, something extremely static, Resnais had a field day with camera movements, low angle tracking shots. There was nothing off-hand about this; on the contrary, it's a question of a highly lucid and intelligent use of methods that could give cause for alarm. The Dyaliscope company helped us a lot technically. In particular they made me, I still have them, the bifocal lenses I used in *Marienbad* to get certain depth-of-field effects.[24]

Philippe Brun recalled that

> It's in this film that I did one of the most difficult shots of my life. We
> began with Albertazzi in very big close-up beside a mirror in which
> two actors were reflected. We had a lens attachment called a *bonnette*, a
> bifocal lens which enables you to have a sharp face in the foreground
> and sharp backgrounds. This is what you do: you line up a vertical at
> the centre of the image with the *bonnette*, you focus it at 12 and the lens
> gives you Albertazzi's face in the focal plane; behind him the wall is
> out-of-focus, but in the mirror the two actors are sharp. All that's at
> the beginning of the shot. After that the camera dispenses with the
> *bonnette*. The actors were coming and going as one slowly pulled back
> in this Amalienberg salon, which had to be an octagonal salon with
> cant-walls. We were shooting with a BNC, a Mitchell camera with a
> clear viewfinder, that's to say with parallax. We had thirty camera
> positions, and the viewfinder's lack of precision made things very
> difficult.[25]

According to Henri Colpi, the chief editor, the final shooting script
was so well-organised that the editing went without a hitch and there
were only a few 'dodgy' moments, one of which was the sequence
shifting back and forth between bar and bedroom.[26] In actual fact,
although the shooting script was extremely precise, in terms of detail
there was a significant amount of improvisation during the shooting.
Delphine Seyrig is eloquent on this:

Seyrig improvising

Contrary to what many people think, *Marienbad* isn't a prefabricated film in which everything was arranged in advance. Certain gestures which seem highly studied are simply the result of my awkwardness. Many scenes were improvised on the spot. I'm thinking, for instance, of the one where I roll against the bedroom mirrors. We didn't know, on the actual morning of the filming, what we were going to do. I wandered about the room, trying out gestures, poses, until Alain said: 'That one, that's good.'[27]

Francis Seyrig, the composer, was brought into things 'a good month too late'. He wrote the music between 20 February and 28 March, beginning with 'the stronger passages, the fifth and seventh reels'. He had photos of each shot at his disposal, 'which enabled me to make a diagram with coloured pencils, to control the musical themes, revert back to them again, etc.'.[28] After first thinking of Versailles, the recording of the organ was finally made at the Louvre Oratory, with Marie-Louise Girod as the soloist. During certain passages a delicate sound mix of organ and orchestra music had to be undertaken.[29]

The Music

The music was one of the things that deeply divided Resnais and Robbe-Grillet. The latter considered that the music Resnais wanted

> didn't add much, except that in the event it found great favour. I, on the other hand, had described a music to set one's teeth on edge. Instead of this beautiful, captivating continuity, I was after a structure of absences and shocks; with percussive elements in the widest sense, not just drums and cymbals. I'd imagined a composition based on the essentially real noises one hears in a hotel, in particular in an old-fashioned hotel like that one. Lift doors, for instance, those metal doors on hinged rods that make a very beautiful sound if properly recorded; or then again the ringing of different bells: the porter's, the chambermaid's, etc., more or less strident or distant; and the whole thing composed with footsteps, isolated notes, shouts.

It's obvious that the writer and director didn't understand the word 'music', as used in cinema, in exactly the same way. Resnais is not someone without his own ideas about music, and hence on the way to utilise it in a film. He has, indeed, a reputation for this. The 50s were in fact musically very interesting and there's no doubt that Resnais closely followed what was being written at the time in this area. The decade began with Oliver Messiaen's *Quatre études de rythme pour piano*. The second of these studies had an enormous influence on the younger generation of musicians. A friend of Messiaen's, André Jolivet, created a *Concerto pour piano et orchestre* (1951) and a *Concerto pour harpe et orchestre* (1952), while Henri Dutilleux composed two *Symphonies* (1951 and 1959). Jean Barraqué's *Sonate* (1952) was one of the major serial scores of the post-war period. Among the orchestral works of the time by Messiaen, one should note *Réveil des oiseaux* (1953) and *Oiseaux exotiques pour piano et petit orchestre* (1956), a work commissioned by Pierre Boulez for the Domaine musical concerts he set up in 1954. The first two seasons took place at the Petit-Marigny theatre. The public was able to hear works by Webern, Schoenberg, Varèse, Messiaen, selections from Stravinsky and Debussy. Boulez decided to apply the serial concept to all kinds of sound; in 1957 he composed his *Troisième sonate pour piano*, in which he ventured onto the terrain of the aleatory. In 1959 he settled in Germany. Concurrently, Pierre Scaeffer and his Concrete Music Ensemble took off in another direction. The 50s saw the creation of important works by Hans Werner Henze and by Karlheinz Stockhausen, who followed Messiaen's teaching in 1952–3 at almost the same moment as Iannis Xenakis, who developed his theory of random music in 1956. During the same period a number of Benjamin Britten operas were mounted.

The use of the organ on the soundtrack was Resnais's idea. He'd thought of asking Oliver Messiaen to compose the music for his film. The latter politely declined the offer. The director then consulted his friend Pierre Barbaud, the musician on *Le Mystère de l'atelier quinze* (1957) and *Le Chant du Styrène* (1958),[30] 'to whom, for months on end, he plays a number of very different works: for example an opera by the Swedish composer Blomdahl. Barbaud thinks he's understood: he proposes Xenakis. The idea doesn't work out.'[31] Resnais finally got in touch with Francis Seyrig, a Messiaen student. Seyrig would say:

> At the beginning I didn't really understand what he was after. He went all around the houses and didn't seem to know exactly what it was he wanted. He'd told me, right off, to do something extremely modern. For three weeks we tried things out on the organ, using the low notes,

then the high. He listened, we discussed it. In the end I realised that he wanted Wagnerian touches for the love-story side of the film, but also a 1925 feel, plus modern bits, all mixed together.[32]

Resnais wanted 'functional' but also lyrical music, the sound curve of which would reproduce that of the film. This image of the curve, of its plotting so to speak, is essential: it is something which seemed to obsess Resnais, and which functions as a connecting thread in the 'scenario' of *L'Année dernière à Marienbad*. Music was needed that would blend with the décor. It's certain that Jacques Saulnier helped crystallise the visual conception of the décor for Resnais:

> One day I showed him a photo of the private apartments of the Crown Prince in Schönbrunn, with German-style wainscoting, the sinusoidal forms of which interested him a lot. We constructed a somewhat wider cornice with *oeils-de-boeuf* at the top, but the overall shape completely respected this sinusoidal form. So I took off from this idea. We devised some panels and reworked certain sculptures which were carved in these panels, the motif of which made him think, he said, of the repetition of a musical phrase.[33]

The film had encountered its form, then, its space and its rhythm. It was the assumption of this decorative aspect which helped the connection with the writing to function, the 'magnificent handwriting' of the letters from Turkey and of the scenario that Resnais must sometimes have visually hallucinated, just as he auditively hallucinated Robbe-Grillet's language: 'I needed a sound. Robbe-Grillet's language sounds magnificent, it hypnotises you. It's true music. I reckon there must be forty minutes of speech in *Marienbad*. It could almost be sung. It's like an opera libretto with very beautiful and very simple words, which are endlessly repeated.'[34] The strength of *L'Année dernière à Marienbad* lies in its having been imagined by Resnais, between statuary and opera, sinusoidal form and abstraction: 'I think one can arrive at a cinema without psychologically defined characters, in which the play of emotions would be in motion, as in a contemporary painting where the play of forms contrives to be stronger than the anecdote.'

27

4

. . . .

A DESCRIPTION OF THE FILM

All Stories Together

Let's not forget that *L'Année dernière* could have been a detective film. Something would remain of that initial project – beginning with a silhouette of Hitchcock glimpsed during one shot. Trails and false trails, royal roads and culs-de-sac all go to make up the scenario of the film. A journalist was to remark in Resnais and Robbe-Grillet's presence that there was often a character looking attentively off-screen in the film. Resnais commented: 'That's Robbe-Grillet's Piero della Francesca side. There's always a figure in Piero della Francesca who's looking beyond the frame.'[35] Robbe-Grillet himself declared that it was in daily life that they'd detected these kind of looks and discussed them. To which we might add that such looks are very frequent in the films of Antonioni, and that Piero della Francesca would be one of Godard's references in *Le Mépris* (1963).

There are three main characters in the hotel setting: a woman (A) and two men (X and M). M is perhaps her husband and X her lover. X wants to persuade the woman that they've already met the year before and that at that time she'd promised to leave with him a year later, that is, 'now'. The woman resists this extremely unusual attempt at seduction. All the questions are posed in relation to this schema: is one of the characters telling the truth? Did they really meet? If so, was seduction involved? Or rape? Did she promise? Is she pretending to have forgotten? Has she really forgotten? Is M her husband? Her brother? Is there incest here? And so on. Robbe-Grillet was to insist:

> The questions you were most likely to ask yourself were: did this man and this woman really meet and fall in love last year in Marienbad? Does the young woman remember and merely pretend not to recognise the handsome stranger? Or has she indeed forgotten everything that has passed between them? Etcetera. Let's get one thing straight: these questions have no meaning.

We can, furthermore, recount the story of the film in another way. In a place which is not unlike a kind of limbo, midway between life and death, a number of human beings, isolated from the world and to all intents and purposes dead, pass their time in idle and repetitive pursuits. A man (X) comes in search of a woman he knew a year before, while she was alive and well; he tries to convince her that she is still alive and that she must go with him in order to escape this baleful world. Still ensnared in that world, she resists, and he lets himself be gradually caught in the trap. As an adjunct to this interpretation, the story echoes that ancient Breton legend in which, after a year's stay of execution, Death comes looking for its victim. More than one detail suggests this: the immobile servants, 'doubtless long since dead'; the compliment addressed to the woman, 'You seem lively'; or the statement she makes, 'You're like a shadow'; or there again, this fragment of a couple's conversation, 'We live like two coffins side by side in the frozen ground of a garden'; and in one of the very last images as, framed in the distance X and A go off together, the curtains around the door under

The immobile servants: 'doubtless long since dead'

Curtains like the drapes of a catafalque

The waltz: an intimation of mortality

which they pass are like the drapes of a catafalque. And not to overlook the very slow waltz (which recurs three times), since it's known that Resnais, who likes this movement a lot, finds it sinister and disturbing, an intimation of mortality.

The name of the play to be performed in the luxury hotel is *Rosmer*, 'an allusion to Ibsen's *Rosmersholm*, a play about father–daughter relations that Freud and Rank judged to be incestuous', according to Robert Benayoun,[36] who sees here the hallmark of Robbe-Grillet who'd imagined the figure of M with grey hair. Given that the title doesn't appear in the screenplay, and that M has jet-black hair in the film, it must be assumed that Resnais had something to do with it, thus retaining (perhaps) a trace of the writer's original intention, and dropping in a more secret, secondary reference to Ibsen: *When We Dead Awaken*, or *Ghosts* are fitting titles for the film.[37] As in *Ghosts*, the source of the action in *Rosmersholm* is the human world haunted by the emphatic presence of the absent/present dead. The presence of the dead Felice becomes stronger and stronger as the play goes on. The following phrase uttered by one of the characters – 'I fear we'll soon be hearing ghosts spoken of' – is perfectly consonant with *L'Année dernière à Marienbad*. On top of that, Ibsen's play enables us to establish a link between this and another of Resnais's films: the fascination exerted in the play by the mill-race and the river announce a similar fascination for the fast-flowing waters of *L'Amour à mort*.[38]

We can be sure of Resnais and Robbe-Grillet's consensus that 'this man and this woman only begin existing when they appear on screen for the first time; prior to that they're nothing; and, after the projection is over, they're nothing once again.' Each person can and must interpret the film in his/her own way. To begin with, it can be argued there have been as many films as there were collaborators. Beginning with Robbe-Grillet: what images did he have in mind while he was putting his text together? And Resnais, what was he seeing in his mind's eye while Robbe-Grillet was working on the script?

Certain of these 'mental' films grew out of the needs of the job: the diagram the script supervisor Sylvette Baudrot drew up, for example, which in both its 'short' and 'long' versions has since become famous (it's been reproduced in *Cahiers du Cinéma*). A lack of chronological indications led her to elaborate the diagram, organising data according to an X and Y axis:

> On the *X-axis*, from left to right, the small black rectangles represent the sequences in the order they appear on the screen, each of which can have several shots (there are 430 shots, spread over 120 sequences). Each rectangle corresponds to a change of set: the 'gallery corridors' (shots 1 to 18), the theatre (19 to 39), the 'twin corridors' (shot 40), the Schleissheim hallway (41), and so on. Also indicated are the three main roles (A, X and M) and the number of their costume, plus the presence, or otherwise, of extras. On the *Y-axis*, the three main areas represent time: at the bottom the present, at the top the past (last year), and in between an intermediary area which has helped me graphically separate the present from the past more clearly, and which represents what one might call 'time in general' (in his shooting script Resnais spoke of 'eternity' shots). Lined up in the middle, these emphatic black touches were to represent shots that had no precise date, everything that was future time or timeless.[39]

This 'time in general' series would, according to Bernard Pingaut, group together a 'succession of static views, or travelling shots along the corridors, shots of promenades in the garden – dead time, a sort of pure description escaping the rigorous order of the narrative'.[40] The contingency which, of itself, was to lead to finding a classification for the shots and to situating them in time leads, finally, to one of the possible interpretations of the film.

A further film is the one elaborated in the minds of the actors, according to how they envisaged their characters. Delphine Seyrig thought that the role of the young woman wasn't natural for her: 'I felt completely alien in the middle of the vast hotel described in the film. ... It was necessary, then, that I completely invent the character.'[41] The amusing part of the whole affair is that one of the extras, Karin de Towarnicki, a Dior model, exactly represents the character as the actress imagined her. Accompanied by the director, Seyrig trawled around the fashion houses. Finally, they lighted on a Chanel evening dress which they then had shortened, playing on the contrast between the 'evening dress' concept and the 'cocktail dress' length. This detail, which draws attention to a hesitation (an 'as well'), is characteristic of a more general hesitancy affecting all the elements making up the film, be they narrative, decorative, descriptive, etc.

Setting

Setting plays a huge part in Robbe-Grillet's most important works. True to his own ideas, the writer thus began with the setting of a grand internation-al hotel, a closed world made up of visual illusion and corridors leading nowhere. This setting was to give rise to the story. In Germany Resnais, as is his habit, took photos, those famous 'location shots' which for Jorge Semprun evoked the works of the photographer Eugène Atget, pictures with a 'scene of the crime' feel to them, it has been said. Resnais asked Jacques Saulnier to note down the shots of the different places they passed through in order to reflect at greater leisure and, perhaps, to 'detect the crime and pick out the guilty party'. Ghosts were to emerge from the preci-sion of these shots and hypnotic contemplation of the resulting photographs. Ghosts like the hotel's female 'prisoner', a clothed version of an 'O' (Marienbad, O's town) Robbe-Grillet imagined to be involved in incest or rape. (Resnais associated her with the long-suffering belles the cinema has brought to life, such as Elizabeth Russell in films produced by Val Lewton.) The setting itself would beget the characters, their postures. Thus it is that the curve of A's neck and shoulder echoes the twisting of the banister against which she stands.

This setting was judiciously chosen, as Jean-Louis Bory has remarked, because it was in fact twofold:

> Mouldings, dadoes, friezes, cornices, astragals and festoons ... the baroque sensuality of the *interior* architecture and decoration of the grand hotel-palace contrasts with the *exterior* Cartesianism of the formal gardens – or rather, there is a play between them. *L'Année*

dernière à Marienbad is based on the kind of play which opposes, to the Cartesianism of conscious life, the baroque nature of our memory and our affective life.

This opposition exists but it is precise up to a point. In effect interior and exterior contaminate one another. For example, two kinds of moulded doors exist, those that hark to the Baroque and those that reproduce the ground plan of the formal garden as seen on the engraving: two paths in the form of a cross, with a rotunda at the centre. The painter Giorgio de Chirico has spoken of the effect produced on him by the Parc de Versailles, where every tree has been formed and deformed by man and where, at the turn of a path, an immobile, gesticulating baroque statue is encountered. We will recognise, furthermore, an echo in the film of this painter in the perspectives which pose insoluble problems for the frozen figures preceded by long shadows. The hotel is, in a sense, peopled by 'metaphysical' mannequins.

The garden with its painted shadows 'was [Resnais's] idea, a precise image he had in mind from the start; it merely needed executing'.[42] It wasn't possible for the film to be shot entirely on location. The studio sets included, according to Jacques Saulnier, 'a sixty-metre-long corridor, which we were able to construct by joining two stages together, other shorter corridors, intersecting, and the bedroom – to begin with, there were two of these – in different states of decoration. It was in the studio that we also shot certain "inserts", such as the scene of the pistol shot with its false ceiling in trompe-l'oeil.'[43] Sylvie Baudrot, the script supervisor, has a telling anecdote:

In *Marienbad*, for example, there was a very long scene in which Delphine Seyrig and Albertazzi walk side by side down a corridor. We shot it in three different corridors, and to make things even more complicated, it was intended to be a continuity scene for the dialogue as well as for the rhythm. We shot one section in a castle at Nymphenburg, another section in a castle at Schleissheim, and the third section, which in fact came first in the order of the film, we filmed in the studio at the end of shooting. We'd put potted plants so that the continuity between the potted plants might disguise the passage from one section of corridor to another, but Resnais didn't want to hide the fact that three different corridors were involved.[44]

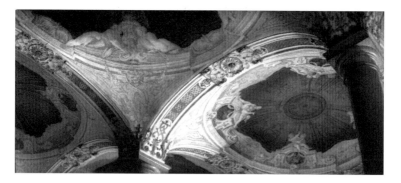

The baroque ceiling in the opening shot

A funereal succession of doors

Posture mimics décor

Inside and outside merge

The *trompe-l'oeil* image with chessboard pattern

The garden with painted shadows

Resnais's ambition here reveals a sought-after effect: a setting that undergoes a transformation, plus a continuity within movement, and modulation. This is the reason the bedroom mantelpiece changes from one moment to the next: a mirror here, a snowy landscape there (an allusion to Ludwig II of Bavaria which doesn't appear in the screenplay). This is why a camera movement can begin with a character and re-encounter him/her at the end of the shot dressed differently, or doing something else, since transformation and modulation affect both characters and objects: the Marienbad game is played with cards, matchsticks, dominoes or photographic images.

Robbe-Grillet specified that on the walls there would be 'old-fashioned engravings representing a formal garden with geometric lawns, bushes trimmed into cones, pyramids, etc., gravel paths, stone balustrades, statues in mildly emphatic poses on massive cubic plinths'. In accordance with these instructions, Resnais had strewn the hotel décor with representations of this garden, which served to decorate the walls. They encourage the idea that there's no longer an inside or an outside, only spaces imbricated in each other. We may swing between one and the other because the exterior is included in the interior, and the perspectival view from the paths of the chateau leads either towards infinity or towards the chateau's façade. At the moment 'the man who is perhaps the husband' explains the subject of the sculpture in the park represented in the engraving, the characters are framed from the point of view of this engraving (that is, from the wall it's on) with, in the background, a *trompe-l'oeil* image taking in the balustrade skirting the statue, and behind that, on the floor, a chessboard pattern (black-and-white squares) which is, it seems, halted by a balustrade similar to the one in the foreground, behind which the chessboard-patterned floor continues once more. The characters are caught like prisoners between the engraving and the dovetailing perspectives which face it. Inside the hotel we re-encounter then the alternative present at the very end of the garden paths: either an infinity we get lost in, or the hotel façade 'from which there is no means of escape'.

The Gaze and the Voice

Like other great directors, Resnais's œuvre has its unresolved, and long-cherished, projects which have ended up serving as 'fuel' for other films. The best-known are *Les Aventures de Harry Dickson*, which Resnais contemplated and worked on from 1951–66, and *Délivrez-nous du bien*, a Richard Seaver script on the life of the Marquis de Sade. In this film one was to insistently hear, in 'a sort of totalising recitative', Sade's voice, 'sometimes almost inaudible … rarely synchronous with the image'. 'The scenic device conceived for the film as a whole, which was to have occupied an entire sound stage, is made up of a sort of labyrinth of scaffolding, permitting the characters to cross, at a preordained point, different spatial zones which form a series of successive and simultaneous locations underpinning the action.' A décor and a 'recitative' which incline the cinema towards both theatre and music: this is the project of *L'Année dernière à Marienbad* as Resnais conceived it.

At the very beginning of the film, after some brisk and over-emphatic music, a hollow voice, at times perceptible, at times not, is heard, interspersed with chords struck on the organ. The voice, penetrating the tympanum of our ear, bids us to enter the labyrinth of which it speaks, while we see a décor for losing oneself in. It asks us to listen and obliges us to follow its fragile spiralling, like an Ariadne's thread in a maze. This voice, which we will discover belongs to the Stranger, at first belongs to no one. It's like the woman's voice at the beginning of *The Secret Beyond the Door* (1947) – an interior voice, a murmur, a rising of the curtain, a setting sail.

The voice speaks of a luxurious, labyrinthine and carceral cultural space; an exceedingly beautiful, funereal and deserted prison. To what use is this setting put? In a sense this prologue sets out the 'atmosphere of the question'. This atmosphere is not an origin, but rather a point of departure and, above all, a constant point of reference. The atmosphere of a work consists in the work's open nature and its rapport with the reader. The film then proceeds to meander beneath the ceilings, along the walls, across rooms, etc., while the voice drones on. We're led somewhere, something is said (murmured). A fourfold question: where are we being led? What is being said (the words aren't always audible, phrases seem to be repeated)? Who is speaking? And who is leading us?

A man (the voice is male) speaks in the first person of a journey that has already been undertaken, apparently, many times. The text seems to conform to the idea of a frieze, or a garland: it 'unwinds' like a frieze with recurring motifs. Such a repetition is produced in various aspects of the décor: a succession of doors, one corridor after the other. Thematically, it emphasises the funereal (lugubrious, black, dark, silent, deserted, empty, sombre, cold, oppressive). All these terms suggest the tomb. The idea of the funerary is linked to that of antiquity – 'edifices and ornamental styles from another century', 'ancient leaf-work' – and here this means an ornamentation which a single adjective describes (and historically specifies, at least from the viewpoint of the history of style): baroque. 'Nature' is absent, or stone-like. We are, indeed, in the world of culture. After Austrian and Bavarian baroque comes Italian (which the foreign accent of the male voice conveys), the land of culture *par excellence*, and before long Norwegian. A camera leads us towards a room where a theatrical representation is drawing to a close.

Is the journey described being undertaken by the owner of this voice? The spectator is led to form that hypothesis, but there's nothing to back it up with any degree of certainty. The gaze meandering through this décor lacks a recognisable human origin. The voice also meanders, now very close to the camera, now moving away (or it's the camera which moves away or comes back to the source of the sound); the voice doesn't belong to a body. The gaze and the voice are adrift of each other. Added to which there is the distance. The voice says, 'As if the ear itself were very far, far from the ground, the carpets, very far from this empty and oppressive décor, very far from this complicated frieze running around the ceiling.' Very far, but where then? And shouldn't the question of the ear be referred to the voice to the gaze? The voice at once audible, then inaudible; at times it is obscured by the music, systematically so, even.

We pass from the dead man's gaze (the framing of Dreyer's *Vampyr* [1932], in the famous scene from this film) to that of someone who might be floating slightly above the ground. In the foreground 'at human height', as in a mirror, we see the film's first human figure in the distance: she advances front-on towards the camera. The decorations in the form of sculptures themselves invite the human figure into shot. A further important new element is obviously the engraving representing the garden: as if the human figure and a setting (we know this is a hotel) were being gradually set in place at one and the same time. A third element is introduced: the announcement of a play. A voice searches for its physical form; this is why it seeks a place and a dramatic situation to be in.

The camera movements continue. The quest is not over. Now we penetrate the blackness, pass through a mirror. Faces loom out of the

Faces looming from the darkness, turned to the left …

… except for the man who may be the husband …

… and the woman on stage, fixed like a statue

39

darkness, attentive and rigid. They are listening: they prolong, then, the idea of an all-powerful voice (in the beginning was the Word) which gives rise, in effect, to the spectator-listeners (or potential 'actors-out'?). The screenplay says 'The faces are elicited from the shadows by the very play they are observing,'[45] posing the problem of origins once more: was the screenplay a product of the cinema beam, before providing the matter to fill this beam? Or is it the other way round? What beam of light do the two *L'Année dernière à Marienbad* issue from? The question posed at the start of the film bears a double origin: that of gaze (camera movement as gaze) and that of voice (a voice embodied in a body), and not that of 'plot' in the classical sense. On one side, a machine; on the other, a human body. The body, like the machine, is invisible.

The Word (the author, in fine) 'descends' in a gaze and a voice which, once embodied, will be dissociated: even though attributed to a fictitious being, the gaze is always that of a machine. The fictitious being endowed with a voice, even reduced to the idea of a character, always possesses the body of a recognisable, and at times identifiable, human being.

We advance towards these characters, then move away from them. A change in camera direction announces a further change: the characters are shown turned to the left, sitting down and cut off at the chest, apart from the man who is perhaps the husband and the woman on the stage: both are standing, turned to the right, which of necessity suggests a relationship between them. The 'husband' appears at the moment the voice says, 'Among whom I too was already waiting for you,' as if this voice were coming from this body. The formal 'you' would be the woman on the stage. The situation itself 'is embodied': a pause. The scene ends on a question posed by the male voice: 'Are you coming?' There exists, then, an interlocutor, or an interlocutrice. In the screenplay we hear the actress before we see her. Resnais proceeds inversely: he shows her, then we hear her (without seeing her). It isn't certain that the voice belongs to the body. It is necessary to wait a little longer before having proof of it. The actress is immobile, fixed in a pose, rendered as a statue or frozen in a single gesture as in a snapshot.

The Theatre: A Film in Search of its Characters
That the first image of a woman is that of an actress (that is, from the theatre, an art of 'rehearsal' [*répétition*] *par excellence*) is interesting on

more than one account: in addition to her skill with make-up and disguise, her faculty for slipping into different roles, the actress presents the peculiarity of being fascinating, idealised, transformed by the footlights, and thus endowed with the sort of magical power the theatre confers on her. Utimately she is two people. In the theatre the actors are not the only ones wearing costumes, the play also extends to the auditorium: the theatre is the setting for a ritual attended in ceremonial dress, a veritable disguise which, given its artificial aspect, transfigures the spectator.

In this narrative the real is never present, it never will be present: it is always a simple 'echo' of the past. The past itself will never be present, either, since it was itself already circumscribed by one phantasm or another, already transformed into some ghostly figure. In theatrical terms the 'rehearsal' is different to the 'revival' [*reprise*]: rehearsals, where the same text is recited in order to demonstrate the mechanism of memory, differ from the revival, where it's a question of an authentic recreation of the play. The same could be said of the reprise in the musical sense of the word. The word *rehearsal* evokes a similitude in the reproduction of word or gesture; *revival* is a second beginning, a new life.

As for the setting, certain of its features are clear enough: the garden path with its rows of shrubbery, a balustrade, a statue. Some features recur which have already appeared in the engraving in the corridor. We realise that a serial order is being set up which obliges us to shift from one type of representation to another: from the engraving to the theatre set (which resembles the backdrops nineteenth- and early twentieth-century photographers placed behind the people whose image they were taking), pending the shift to a third type of representation, intended to refer to the 'real' – a real which will be necessarily contaminated by these earlier representations.

Intercut with the shots of the spectators is one which takes in the actor, the actress's interlocutor. This plan is unique in the way it begins (the descending movement which first takes in the top of his skull); also unique is this head seen face-on, with its searching and almost alarming look, like a predator fixing on its victim (a vampire, one would say). It's an apparition. While the actress is placed within a décor, he isn't: the background behind him is uniformly black, as it is to the rear of the spectators, although he, unlike them, sports a white bow-tie. And just as the actress was associated with M, he is associated with a female spectator (towards whom a forward tracking shot is made, similar to the one towards the actress). Immediately following this female spectator we re-encounter the 'husband' (presented in the inverse manner to his first appearance; that is, with a forward movement of the camera). In this way the woman is now actress, now spectator; her male opposite also occupies these two positions. And behind the two actors on the stage their shadow reduplicates them.

This passage is without music. The chiming of the clock introduces time (or at least a sign of time): '*Now*, I am yours.' At that moment the actress on stage lowers her hand as if coming out of trance. This shot of her is static at first, then there's a pan to the left as she makes a turning movement; the pan reveals the man on the left. In the screenplay the actress remains perfectly still. The movement creates an effect that will often occur in the film: the character doesn't look in the direction of his interlocutor; he looks even in the opposite direction, hence the impression of a confused space. Another effect relies on the presence of the actor on the left of the frame: this presence is all the more surprising since there was nobody there before and there has been no entry on-stage. The feeling of witnessing an apparition is thereby reinforced.

This moment implies a series of shifts. For instance, the changeover of the voice heard since the beginning to that of the actor's on stage (who repeats the same text; it's the first time we see lips moving). Time is constantly invoked in the actor's lines: 'a few minutes, a few seconds … still, already … in future, for always.' Loss, expectancy, fear, hope, encounter, hesitation: all these 'themes' are set out, just as the location is confirmed ('this hotel', 'a past represented in marble, like these statues, this garden hewn in the rock').

The text tells us that we're at the end of the play: 'the story is done.' An end and a beginning. The light from the stage has brought the room to life and the nature of this play, its content, can now be extended into the room. 'I am yours' is spoken during a shot showing the stage from the room, as if the real interlocutor was there and not here; the formulation itself is ambiguous.

At first the theatre stage is seen from the room, yet it is as if the room itself is seen by someone 'in the background'; then the room is seen from the stage. The room is thus caught between these two points of view. Henceforth the hotel, which has been shown as being empty, will seem, at least in the places shown, to be occupied by a great many

The view from the stage

residents (assembled in small groups). The presence in the décor of three windows in an arc and the fact that the characters are, when not in pairs, presented in a triangular composition, suggest that the story will crystallise around a threesome, as the text spoken on stage has already suggested.

Among these spectators we can see A, played by Delphine Seyrig, lost in thought at the extreme right of the frame (in fact she is seen three times, far off and indistinct). The script allows for 'shooting' around her, having her emerge slowly. Her folded arm posture is repeated by a blonde woman. A difference is noticeable here between the screenplay and the film: one names, the other shows. During her first appearance in the screenplay A is repeatedly seen among the spectators, as in the film: the fact of naming her is very different from showing her over and again, always at the edge of the frame, unidentifiable as long as we don't know who she is, the more so when a forward travelling shot on a young woman in front of her seems to set this character apart (as if the choice of female lead hadn't already been made, that it could just as easily be this other woman).

We hear voices, we see mouths opening – or not. What these voices insist on, however briefly, is the idea of temporal confusion ('in '28 or in '29'), the former meeting (we've already met) and the suspended narrative (the outcome wasn't known). The mismatching of image and sound (as far as the spoken word is concerned) is systematic. It is systematic throughout the film: the sound of footsteps on gravel as a

Groups of three, A at the edge of the frame

Antonioni and della Francesca: characters look in opposite directions and beyond the frame

character climbs the stairs; organ music while the musicians in the image are playing string instruments. Added to which the characters seem to stand still, as if once endowed with bodily form they have difficulty moving.

All of a sudden the music stops – such sudden breaks in the music often occur in the film – on a shot in which we've visibly changed space. We're no longer in the room where the theatrical presentation took place. In the background we see a corridor down which two silhouetted figures are headed. A man at the centre of the frame turns to face (when, like the others, he was looking towards the left) something we don't see. This movement makes the character stand out (it's the first such brusque movement) and creates the illusion of a potential match cut: what is he looking at? Might he not have turned his head because the music stopped? This shot is perhaps the first of a series, described thus in the screenplay: 'In this series new groups must be interpolated which do not appertain to the theatre auditorium, but to other rooms in the hotel and at some other moment. Hence, after the images of the theatre there follows a series of views of the hotel and of the characters in it, a bit everywhere, a bit at all times.'[46]

There are various changes of space: to the hotel lobby, an unidentifiable location. These are linked to the theatre, the first by the left-to-right movement of a woman in the background, the second by the presence of an identical character in the foreground (the blonde woman). In the cinematic tradition an identical character in different clothes may appear in the same space (in *Duck Soup* [1933] or in musical comedies), or indeed a single, identical character traverses different locations (Buster Keaton in *Sherlock Jr.* [1924]). The sequence develops the movement by which a character turns round – or has already turned (the match cut is even made at the end of this movement); the other figure is the Antonionian one of characters looking in opposite directions. A number of previously seen characters (the bald man, the two blonde women) recur; we circle around couples or threesomes; changes happen on the soundtrack. This moment is wordless (even though the lips move); a confused murmur recurs when the woman turns round – this sound 'event' does not exist in the screenplay. These differing events will be reproduced in the film.

'A bit everywhere, a bit at all times,' is a phrase of Robbe-Grillet's. The 'a bit everywhere' aspect is illustrated yet, despite everything, we situate the images that follow in a temporal continuity, 'after' the play. There is the feeling of a soirée drawing to a close: the people return to their rooms, the hotel empties. We revert to the initial desertedness.

We start off with an unknown person, then the 'husband' appears among the other spectators, looking at two actors on a theatre stage at the moment the voice says 'Among whom I too was already waiting for you.' When the man in whom the voice is embodied appears, it is at the edge of a large mirror in which there is reflected a far-off couple, exchanging words that the couple will pronounce along with the 'husband'. He looks towards the left, off-screen, the hypothetical place where the couple in the mirror beside him is. The couple draws near, leaves by the door he was

The mirror sequence

standing beside (he has disappeared); a pan towards the left reveals, on the left of the frame, the young woman still lost in thought. The double, symmetrical presentation of this man and the 'husband' is noteworthy because in Robbe-Grillet's text the couple does not appear in the mirror. Resnais, then, has knowingly made a parallel between the couple on the stage and the couple framed in the mirror. In addition Robbe-Grillet doesn't show A close to the mirror, contrary to what happens in the film; another sign of Resnais's desire to establish a symmetry in the presentation of the characters.

The double presentation beside the mirror is effected in a sequence shot which ends on a man looking at the engraving representing the garden. X is alongside him, turns away and goes through a succession of doors which are clearly the hotel equivalent of the paths in the garden. The idea of this shot sequence is Resnais's. It allows for transformation and modulation, and shows the mirror (and is itself the mirror) which 'changes things into images, images into things, myself into the other and the other into myself', to use a formulation of Merleau-Ponty's.

The voice we hear is that of the man next to the mirror, but could it not be attributable, in the first instance, to the 'husband' whose eyes observe the discussion on stage which is (has been, or will be) that of the young woman and the other man? And could the two men not be simply two versions of male desire acting out, around a female figure, the eternal scenario of possession and seduction, of deviousness and jealousy? (Didn't the two Alains act out a similar scenario around the film and the screenplay?) 'X M A' can and must be read as 'X (a man) aime [loves] A (a woman).' As soon as the drive impelling a man towards a woman is evoked, a parthenogenesis follows which renders it impossible to determine who comes first, X or M, each being the mediator of the passion and suffering of the other. As for the young woman, she herself is divided into a beautiful woman clad in black and a woman dressed in white. And so we swing from one man to the other, from film to screenplay, and from a woman in black to a woman in white.

In the film, two characters playing draughts are framed before the *trompe-l'œil* backdrop with its balustraded setting repeated *ad infinitum*, situated opposite the engraving representing the garden and the statue (which isn't described as such by Robbe-Grillet, although it is reproduced in his book as a frame blow-up). It is a question, here, of the 'husband' tactically undermining the other man's plans, of cutting short

Playing draughts in front of the *trompe-l'oeil* background

his incursions into the past by which he tries to capture the young woman. The 'husband' is, furthermore, the one who always wins the 'Marienbad game' (another reason why Robbe-Grillet designates him by the first letter of the spa's name): lucky at cards, unlucky in love. A double game, then, for each of the two men, and signified by the twin receding perspectives: that of the park for the narrator and of the checkerboard for the husband, reversible as they both are, false exits, labyrinths in which one is always brought back to the same places. *L'Année dernière à Marienbad* is undeniably a black-and-white film; it's impossible to think of it in any other form, and the text makes only one reference to colour. This is towards the end, when A announces to M, who has just told her

The 'Marienbad game'

that he'd been vainly searching for her, that she was 'in the little green salon near the music room'. The colour green conjoins two meanings, hope shading into jealousy, beside a room where the sonorous tones of well-tuned instruments are blending in total harmony.

The Statue, 'Mise en abyme' of the Film

The statue near which a famous scene in the film unfolds is characteristic of the play of interpretations the film elicits. As to this statue, the set designer Jacques Saulnier has provided the following information: 'The statue had been made in Paris, then transported to Munich, where it still is. To begin with Resnais was thinking of Max Ernst. He'd even written to him, I believe. Then, inspired by a painting by Poussin, he asked for designs and sketches to be made. Without hurrying, and after discussing each new design, his ideas progressively changed.'[47]

> At first I didn't know what it was or what it was about, nor even if it should be a couple. It was Alain Resnais who had the idea of those two figures in a Poussin painting: two really undecipherable figures in the background. So undecipherable in fact that the sculptor (there were three of them: Grache, his wife and Babinet) asked if it was two men or two women. Jean Léon replied two women. Jacques Saulnier argued for two men. The quarrel was resolved by Resnais, who concluded that it was unquestionably a man and a woman.[48]

Whether the Poussin painting is *La Peste d'Asrod* (or 'd'Azoth'), *Le Miracle de l'Arche dans le temple de Dagon* or *Les Philistins frappés par la*

The statue

peste (a happy accident in this instance, since the title is undecided), of the two figures in profile who could have inspired the statue, one is bearded, which indeed suggests the degree of mimetism the 'paratext' has attained in relation to the text and the film. Or there again ... Another source is the painting, *Achille parmi les filles de Lycomède* (the Richmond Museum version, rather than the Boston one) in which two figures, seen face-on, are bearded.

The woman compared to a statue is an implicit reference to Jensen's story *Gradiva*. In the deserted ruins of Pompeii, at the spectral hour of midday, Norbert Hanold meets a young woman who strangely resembles the figure of a Roman bas-relief he has at home. What strikes him is the movement of her feet:

> The left foot had advanced, and the right, about to follow, touched the ground only lightly with the tips of the toes, while the sole and heel were raised almost vertically. This movement produced a double impression of exceptional agility and of confident composure, and the flight-like poise, combined with a firm step, lent her peculiar grace.

A kind of snapshot, then, between pose and movement. The acting style demanded of Delphine Seyrig was doubtless aimed at recapturing this 'peculiar grace'.

'I told you you had an animated air,' the narrator says to the young woman; he speaks just after the statue in the film. If the humans are 'turned into stone' (by their immobility, poses, rigid gestures, etc.), the statue itself is animated by the shots of it taken from different angles; it changes location, like the fake balustrade which is found in different places in the film. The technique of montage also permits *rapprochements* and oppositions to be made; finally, many interpretations of the subject of the sculpture are put forward, just as many representations of it are offered: in words, in an engraving ...

One of the hands of the female figure in the statuary group is extended, while her other hand rests on the man's shoulder. A reversal: the man's hand is extended towards the young woman ('Please ... '), while the latter places her hand on his shoulder. The words of the two men, the displacement of the elements making up the statue (the figures with their particular hairstyles, clothes and gestures, and the dog accompanying them which nobody knows what to do with) to the engraving or to the heroine's and narrator's poses create a number of intersecting systems and a somewhat serial composition.

Suzanne Liandrat-Guigues believes that the film presents, through the intermediary of differing interpretations of the statuary,

> the inextricable web of time. The statue is ageless. Its existence is recent. It is a simulacrum, a copy (like the statuary in *Le Mépris*), and it is clearly an adaptation of a detail from a visual work. Its function in the film seems to be to encourage interpretation or identification, to incite the characters to imagine things. It helps make the film a consistently open work. Like the theatre stage, the statue clearly suggests the idea of representation, but also that of the many combinations of game imagery which feature in the film. ... Beginning with the conflict of interpretations and of the aleatoriness of memory, the statue sets different conceptions of time against each other: 'The eternal instant of Marienbad is divided between a now-imaginary past and an as-yet unimagined future.' For all these reasons, the statue is really the *mise en abyme* of the film, not least because Resnais wanted, at the time, to make a film which is looked at as if it were a sculpture.[49]

5

THE TWO 'L'ANNÉE DERNIÈRE À MARIENBAD'

A Pair of Twin Works

Traditionally, a script has a particular status which is not that of an entirely separate work. It's a document, a stage to be gone through. In the case of *L'Année dernière à Marienbad*, things are complicated by the fact that there are two quasi-simultaneous and inseparable works. In effect there are two *L'Année dernière à Marienbad*, a film signed 'Alain Resnais' and a screenplay signed 'Alain Robbe-Grillet'. The two *L'Année dernière à Marienbad* are twin works, at once divergent and complementary. Although at the time the film was sometimes presented as the work of the two Alains (photographs showed the two men in symmetrical poses), it is in fact Resnais's alone, Robbe-Grillet being the author of a screenplay and not a scenario and dialogue script (as with the books of Marguerite Duras, Jean Cayrol, Jorge Semprun and Jacques Sternberg which accompanied the release of *Hiroshima mon amour*, *Muriel*, *Stavisky* and *Je t'aime, je t'aime*). We can opt for knowing only one of the two works, or the two together; in which case we will indiscriminately explore first the one or the other. Whatever the choice, their great proximity (the dialogues are almost identical) and their many infinitesimal or more visible differences will be noted. Robbe-Grillet has said:

> I wrote, not a scenario, but a straightforward shooting script. Next, Resnais did the filming and he filmed solo. He scrupulously respected every detail, to such a degree (I was in Istanbul at the time) that he was sending me a telegram every time he wanted to change a comma in the text. Nevertheless, he has transformed everything; and it's obvious that, while a reading of my work (published in book form) might lead one to believe in the total agreement of the two works, the film is nevertheless by him.

The film isn't an adaptation in the strict sense. Resnais based it on Robbe-Grillet's text, though the two works seem to have more a simultaneous than a chronological relationship, strangely similar yet consistently different (for reasons other than their belonging to different forms of expression). We can enjoy Resnais's film without knowing the screenplay, but knowledge of Robbe-Grillet's work does add another dimension to Resnais's opus. Conversely, it's possible to read the screenplay without knowing the film, but it's impossible to do this without encountering some allusion to the locations it was shot in and without the frame stills that illustrate it (with a reference to the pages where a description of the scene represented can be read). Robbe-Grillet reworked his text after having seen the film, with the result that this written version is also a *reprise*. If Resnais picks up on the echoes the screenplay awakens in him, Robbe-Grillet *tunes* his text to the memory of the initial idea, filtered through a viewing of the film.

The spectator is asked to look and to listen. With tremendous faithfulness the film puts across what we can also read published under the name of Robbe-Grillet, and which preceded its making; the film allows us to see the characters and locations that these words transmuted. Robbe-Grillet's text is instantly anamorphosed through a series of strange voices; and as for Resnais's images, they bear the trace of the descriptions penned by the writer. Robbe-Grillet's words and Resnais's images are presented together, and play on their convergences and their divergences. The writing (the screenplay) is distinguishable from speech, in that writing is definitive while speech is open, uncertain. The writing must also reckon with another rival, the sing-song tone which possesses a particular force of conviction, and is an 'autonomous language' on which Resnais systematically relies: the voices of the three actors with their inflections and their accents sustained by Francis Seyrig's music.

The Credit Sequence

At first Resnais seems to illustrate exactly what Robbe-Grillet has written: violent and tumultuous 'end-of-film' music, a credit sequence of the classic type against a grey background. This, indeed, is what our ears and eyes register. But the Robbe-Grillet description adds: 'Gradually, the edges of the frame are transformed, they become denser, are ornamented with various flourishes which finally form something like picture frames, at first flat, then painted in trompe-l'oeil in such a way as to suggest objects in relief.'[50] Of this there is no trace in the film. The credit sequence we see is visually uniform from start to finish.

Robbe-Grillet had foreseen that 'the music would slowly be transformed into a man's voice'. According to him, the idea was for a double transformation of image and sound. Resnais has not retained the transformation of the image track; this idea makes way for a different one, then. The initial music is heard over the five title cards featuring the actors' names.[51] The sixth title bears the name of the film: organ music and the whispering voice take over (for fourteen titles, until the end of the credits). This procedure foregrounds the idea of an end and a (re)beginning, underlined by the text itself which insists on the 'one more time' aspect; the text begins in *medias res*, in the middle of a sentence, and ends up being obliterated by the music, when it is said that the sound of footsteps is absorbed by the carpets. If we add that this text appears to go back over itself, reprising different notions slightly modified by substitutions (the ear/the footfall of the man; an edifice/ornamentation from another century) and interlocking elements, then we are made aware that the film will consist of the meticulous and obsessional inventory of a limited universe ruled by permutation and repetition – and since the outcome of this spiralling universe of expression will be an excess of contamination – the question comes up again: which one gives rise to the other? For the moment, this involves sound: the voice/the footsteps, the organ/the carpets – we can say that this beginning functions as a true set of instructions.

The Balustrade Scene

The difference most frequently pointed out between the film and the screenplay is Resnais's substitution in the rape episode of a series of 'bleached-out' travelling shots of the young woman. We might also mention the snapping of the bracelet and the lost pearls which Resnais didn't utilise. But rather than to the 'visible' differences it is preferable, in order to

understand the nature of the work Resnais effected on the Robbe-Grillet text, to look to an episode like the one involving the collapsing balustrade.

A single detail demonstrates the sort of difference existing between the two works. The broken balustrade provokes the young woman's cry of alarm, which dissolves to her cry of alarm in the bar. This dissolve might seem arbitrary, governed solely by the logic of the fragment which wants the passage from interior to exterior to be consistent. And yet there's another reason for it: previously in the same bar the 'heroine', stepping back, had bumped into a blonde woman and caused the glass she was holding to fall to the ground, where it broke. Robbe-Grillet's text specifically points to this relationship: 'a large room in the hotel, the ballroom for example, near the bar, on the spot where the scene of the broken glass occurred'. He points to another lead with the indication: 'a long violent cry of terror, or for breaking a spell'. The two works, then,

The end of the rape sequence

M approaches

The broken balustrade

Screaming from where M was

each in its own way, develop a series of associations around the idea of a 'break': the writer plays on both the proper and figurative meaning of the word. Resnais on the other hand appeals to the spectator's recall – a recollection of the film which is obliged to associate two scenes separated in time, plus an intertextual memory, since with the laughter on the soundtrack we recognise, at that moment, the 'illustration' of a Guillaume Apollinaire verse, 'My glass has shattered like a burst of laughter' (from 'Nuit rhénane').

Another detail is the displacement made by Resnais of the 'long falling sound of an imposing mass of large stones, crashing from a great height onto hard ground'. Robbe-Grillet has this sound heard during the shot of M on the path, while the next shot, in which A looks at the collapsed balustrade, 'is perfectly silent'. Between these two shots Resnais inserts a close-up of the young woman (a touch of classical intensity) which he accompanies with the sound of falling stones (very like, in actual fact, that of a tomb closing or opening in a horror film). Robbe-Grillet situates this close-up before M's arrival. Resnais, then, performs a double displacement: that of the two shots whose order is inverted, and that of the sound of one shot made over to another. These transformations are of minor importance in appearance only. M's lack of reaction to the sound of the falling stones does not exist at the point in the film where the arrival of the character seems to provoke the catastrophe. Robbe-Grillet imagines that A's black wrap comes undone at this moment and slips from her shoulder, revealing a white négligé. Resnais doesn't find it necessary to over-emphasise the event; added to which, as he's just shown the young woman dressed in white in various over-exposed shots, he doesn't seek to reinscribe the opposition within the scene.

In the screenplay the shot which follows the one in which A, seen from the back, looks at the collapsed balustrade presents A face-on. Resnais keeps to this principle and accentuates the about-face in two ways: after the shot in which 'he who is maybe the husband' moves towards us, he shows the face of the young woman turning round in close-up, and the shot in which she is face-on reveals, behind her, the space, now empty, where three shots before the hypothetical husband stood; the latter's disappearance transforms his arrival into something ghostly. The film-maker retains the turning-round or the reversal and makes it the most essential part of the sequence: the forward tracking shots become reverse tracking shots, the characters are now inside, now outside, at least in traditional topographical terms (a few shots before, a similar sequence in the hotel accompanies the left turn of the young woman's face in close-up, match cut to the same movement in the park). Robbe-Grillet imagines one continuous movement – 'a long and labyrinthine continous movement, or at least one giving the impression of continuity ... Finally, the movement ends up in the garden at night, and continues there in the same way' – leading from the hotel interior into the park and as far as the place where X is found. Prior to crossing a confined space in the direction of a window Resnais interrupts a forward tracking shot, halting it at the moment when the lateral edges of the French windows and the lower horizontal limit defined by the balustrade (forming a frame) have just disappeared from view. The slowness of the movement and the silence contrast with what comes before, the series of rapid and slower over-exposed tracking shots of the young woman with her arms raised. The perspective view is then shown of the deserted pathway in the park, such as it has been seen many times before (more often than not with a few strollers, or even with various immobile figures, or there again empty but with people in the foreground, now absent), as it is represented in the engravings on the hotel walls, or in the form of a highly stylised negative image, etc. The lesson is clear: either one returns whence one came, or one gets lost. This is the reason Resnais halts his tracking shot before the balustrade edge.

The next shot is described thus by Robbe-Grillet: 'X remains standing ... in profile, with his back possibly against the plinth of a statue ... The camera rotates a quarter turn towards the side X is looking at. X thus exits the frame, while A appears in it, but in the background. The image stops on her: a silhouette enveloped in darkness, immobile, fixedly regarding the camera.' Once again Resnais follows the text faithfully, apart from certain details: the character doesn't exit the frame, so that the shot ends on him and the young woman face to face 'with a few metres between them', both immobile, exactly as the man's voice says. But there is a slight discrepancy: as the voice pronounces the words, 'You were standing in front of me, waiting, unable to take a step forward or back,' the young woman takes a little step forward and comes to a halt. In effect the voice has previously said, 'Having recognised me, you stopped,' which supposes a suspended movement, but the description of the image which should accompany these words gives no indication of movement ('a silhouette enveloped in darkness, immobile'). Resnais's interpretation slips into the interstices of the text. The immobility of the characters does in fact echo, in the man's case, the statuary (as if he were the statue descended from its plinth) and, in the young woman's, the bushes 'trimmed into pyramids' which decorate the edges of the paths. The dark silhouette of the young woman has something of their shape. The only movement is the rippling of the water, or that of the feathers of the heroine's dress which the wind ruffles at her neck.

At the other extreme to the scene of the collapsing balustrade is the young woman's exit from the bar of the ballroom. Robbe-Grillet has a shot of her from the back, moving off 'down an empty corridor'. The film takes liberties with the screenplay: it includes two shots of the young woman ascending a grand staircase, framed laterally and face-on in the first, and taken midway through her ascent (we see neither the top nor the bottom of the stairs) in the second (it appears not to be the same staircase, moreover). At times Resnais flies in the face of Robbe-Grillet's indications. As the novelist has it, in the shot after the characters have been shown face to face, and as stiff as the statues and bushes, X and A are 'closer to one another, now, in the same nocturnal garden, yet in some other place: against a stone balustrade'. Resnais begins this shot with an extremely fast lateral tracking shot following the woman running alongside a balustrade in the man's direction. This movement is consistent with the series of reversals the sequence proposes.

And then there are the things the film includes which the screenplay doesn't, which originate in what one might call the film-maker's room for manoeuvre. The musical accompaniment, for instance, or the heavily emphasised shadows of the characters: the shadows of the man and of 'he who is maybe the husband' on the plinth of the statue; the shadows of the man and the young woman in the high angle shot (from a staircase) in the hotel; the shadow of the young woman on the stairs; her shadow, again, which fleetingly covers the 'husband's' face in the scene in the bar when she is about to exit the frame; or the play of movement on the faces, in close-up, of the man and woman (face-on or in profile, but not always consistently, the profile changing, etc.); the framing of the bar when the 'husband' offers a glass of water to the young woman, now seen from the back (which isn't specified by Robbe-Grillet) opposite the two men who are both face-on; the décor the 'husband' finds himself in when he appears and for which no indication exists in the screenplay – Resnais has the character (who is immobile in the screenplay) walk down a pathway in which the plinths are devoid of statues.

Image and Writing

For André S. Labarthe and Jacques Rivette, come to interview the two authors, the balustrade episode evoked Feuillade. Robbe-Grillet, who claims never to have read the *Fantômas* stories, retorted: 'This image is, though, one that clearly figured in the scenario. So I can hardly have been influenced, as you can see.' The ambiguity here is evidently on the word 'image'. Added to which the novelist makes a pretence of not knowing that 'Feuillade's serials' are films and not novels. Resnais supplied the following detail which apparently backs up the writer's position: 'I remember telling Albertazzi to straddle the balustrade "Arsène Lupin-style". It gave the right atmosphere. And in my opinion this is justified since, in as much as it's an image … clearly projected by the young woman's anguish, it's absolutely normal that, in such circumstances, it might appeal to the tradition of popular novels.' Resnais makes a pretence of speaking of popular fiction, but he's in fact referring to Jacques Becker's film *Les Aventures d'Arsène Lupin* (1957), at the beginning of which Robert Lamoureux bestrides a balustrade. Robbe-Grillet could then add that at this moment the young woman says, 'If you love me, go!', 'which clearly shows just how "theatrical" the scene is!'. This dialogue is, it seems, an illustration of the film-maker's remark in the same interview about the 'images' the two interlocutors possibly have 'in their heads', images which respond to, interfere with, even contradict each other. Furthermore, Resnais reintroduced the difference that existed between the replies he and Robbe-Grillet made to the *Cahiers du Cinéma* critics, namely the reference to cinema and not to literature, in pointing to the regret he felt at 'not having made *Fantômas*'.

The Origins of the Artwork

Being at the origin of two works is something that has happened to Resnais
on other occasions. Years later Henze would compose, with his music for
L'Amour à mort, an 'autonomous' work. In that example, however, identi-
fying the original opus is not at all difficult, whereas with *L'Année dernière
à Marienbad* we are dealing with the simultaneous procreation of two
works, the one engendering the other. One of the two works (but which?)
would be a rewrite of the other; and not just because, using its own means,
the one translates the other. In this particular case, we can put forward the
hypothesis that the rewritten work is neither the film nor the screenplay,
but a third opus predating the other two (which are simultaneous), a truly
original work that must have been forgotten and that the screenplay would
disclose via the film and the film via the screenplay, and which must be one
of the great narratives of European culture, with its own characters, its situations, the emotions its elicits, etc., just as Robbe-Grillet 'reinvents' the
game of Nim, which dates from 3000 BC.

The issue, here, is of the origins of an artwork and of the origins of
cultural memory. 'L'année dernière' is *a priori* that past which, over time,
the present never ceases to repeat. Marienbad is not the place where the
action unfolds (the text has 'here, in this salon', and differentiates between
Fredericksbad, Karlstadt, Marienbad and Baden-Salsa);[52] it is, perhaps,
one of the places where an action is repeated which has already taken place
many times before. It is also a cipher referring to the former glories of a spa
town (at that time in Czechoslovakia) and to those of a vanished Europe
'with its ancient ramparts'. This cipher brings to mind Goethe's *Elegy to
Marienbad* or Adolf Bioy Casares's *The Invention of Morel*, a book based
on the 'eternal' repetition of a situation, which refers explicitly to the
summer residents of Marienbad, and links Bohemia to Bavaria, the Castle
of Nymphenburg to the park in Schleissheim, etc. We are in the temporali-
ty of the eternal return; confronted by the category of repetition. *L'Année
dernière à Marienbad* is built, then, on the repetition of one work within
another, on the theme of repetition related to an uncertain situation (which
has perhaps taken place), and on the recurring presence of places, words,
gestures. As the philosopher remarked, the highest object of art might be
'to have all these repetitions going on at the same time'.[53]

6

....

'L'ANNÉE DERNIÈRE À MARIENBAD' AND THE HISTORY OF CINEMA

Reminiscences

References to other films are not lacking in *L'Année dernière à Marienbad*. Resnais asked the members of his team to go and view or review various films at the Cinémathèque.

> Resnais wanted to rediscover the style of the grand productions of the old days, of those fabulous costumes covered in feathers, boas, the final era of the silents and the beginning of the talkies. He'd shown Bernard Evein photos of L'Herbier films like *L'Inhumaine* and *L'Argent*, the costumes for which were created by the great fashion designers.[54]

Among the films seen again was Pabst's *Pandora's Box* (1928), because Alain Resnais wanted Delphine Seyrig to resemble Louise Brooks in her acting, hairstyle and make-up.[55]

Certain allusions are abundantly clear. It's permissible, in fact, to see in the final shot of the balustrade scene an echo of the stairs in *Destiny* (1921), climbed by the young woman going to her meeting with 'weary Death'. Other allusions are more secret. Hence the text 'through which I was advancing to meet you between two rows of immobile faces' evokes certain previously-seen situations, the man or woman who advances between two rows of immobile faces, as in Cocteau's *La Belle et la Bête* (1946). In *Le Sang d'un poète* (1930) cards are being played around a table: a very beautiful and mysterious woman is present. It would be no surprise were she to haunt the corridors of the Marienbad hotel, along with Louise Brooks and other Fritz Lang or Marcel L'Herbier figures, in a Feuillade light and in the black-and-white of silent film. And since cinema always refers to cinema, doesn't the action unfold in a hospital (the hotel is defined as 'a place of rest') as in *The Cabinet of Dr. Caligari* (1919)?

Modernity

Current discourse applies the notion of modernity to French directors like Jean-Luc Godard or Jacques Rivette, to the detriment of others

L'Inhumaine

L'Argent

India Song

Louise Brooks in *Pandora's Box*

like Alain Resnais. If one takes the word 'modern' to designate what pertains to our most immediate times or, more precisely, that extreme point of contemporaneity which is already oriented towards the future, then one cannot help recognising that, for a dozen years or so, from the mid-50s to the mid-60s, Alain Resnais was undoubtedly the modern film-maker *par excellence*. The special May 1957 issue of *Cahiers du Cinéma*, 'The Current State of French Cinema', opens with a photo of Resnais filming one of the tracking shots from *Toute la mémoire du monde* and asks: 'The French cinema in full momentum?' A few years later Youssef Ishaghpour would call *Muriel* a 'masterpiece of modern cinema'.[56]

To begin with, it can be said that there is no better film than *L'Année dernière à Marienbad* to illustrate the rupture of the sensory-motor schema Gilles Deleuze speaks of when defining the possibilities of a time-image. A film like Marguerite Duras's

India Song obviously owes much to *L'Année*. Closer to it in time, *La Jetée* (Chris Marker, 1962) and *Méditerranée* (Jean-Daniel Pollet, 1963) follow a similar line of investigation. Marker is a friend of Resnais's, they have worked together and it isn't surprising that they might share a similar way of thinking. *La Jetée* relies on a montage of photographs, apart from one shot in which a young woman opens her eyes. Photography isolates things more than cinema does. In *L'Année dernière à Marienbad*, the couple formed by X and A are never physically reunited in real terms, apart from twice beside a stretch of water, when X takes A in his arms and makes as if to caress her breasts. The tenderness and fluidity of these scenes contrast strongly with the distance and coldness which fill the other scenes. Marker was to imagine a similarly fleeting moment of tenderness against a background of generalised immobility.

Méditerranée develops, in relation to a European cultural space far different from Marienbad's, a great many visual or sound repetitions. These series, which are themselves divided into sub-series, group various themes and motifs together, some sixty in all (the list is not infinite, but can always be augmented by a new element). The soundtrack itself has its very own series: different noises (stridulations, the buzzing of flies, water from a fountain or spring, the shouts of the crowd in the arena); musical passages; the text with its repeated words, phrases and expressions. This, as its author Philippe Sollers says, 'doubles' the image, which does not mean that it redoubles it. This Mediterranean 'is in the midst of different lands'; the central region, says Jean-Luc Godard at the end of *Scénario du film Passion*. The film begins with an image of barbed wire (the experience of disaster), then moves on to images of Horus and the Pyramids, while the text speaks of the flight of an 'unknown memory' towards 'more and more distant eras', an expression which is perfectly in keeping with Resnais's film. It evokes an 'other side' behind the curtain, an unimaginable somewhere, a double which stands in for us; a final conjunction is hinted at. On the one hand 'things seen without vision', on the other a duplicating of space, people and movement ('detached from itself'). The mirror suddenly takes on vast importance. Everything is shown twice and in an outward appearance which perhaps relates to thought itself, but which is not of the order of the visible. *L'Année dernière à Marienbad*, then, anticipates *Méditerranée* in more ways than one.

Godard and Resnais

Jean-Luc Godard's *Le Mépris* (1963) clearly owes as much to *L'Année dernière à Marienbad* as it does to Pollet's film: a relationship is woven between Resnais's and Godard's film through the presence of the statues; Cocteau constituted a common reference for the two film-makers. A year after *L'Année dernière à Marienbad* Jean-Luc Godard looked to the same source of inspiration – Louise Brooks – for the Anna Karina character in *Vivre sa vie* (1962). As for the gunfiring scene which appeared twice in Resnais's film, it prefigured a similar sequence in *Alphaville* (1965).

In 1959 Godard argued that Resnais was 'the second greatest editor in the world, after Eisenstein'. A viewing of *Le Chant du styrène* (1958) led him to say that Resnais 'has invented the modern tracking shot'. He ranked *Hiroshima mon amour* among the ten best films of 1959, as he would *Muriel* among the ten best of 1963. Godard, then, valued Resnais very highly. In the 70s, however, he showed himself to be rather more exacting. Nevertheless, it could be argued that the dialogue between the two film-makers has never ended. In 1974 Godard claimed that there were many ways of making films, notably 'like Alain Resnais, who makes sculpture'. This question of sculpture resurfaced in his own work in 1983, with *Prénom Carmen*. The 'forever' formula resonated some years later in *Puissance de la parole* (1988). At the beginning of the opening chapter of his *Histoire(s) du cinéma* (1988) Godard cites two passages from the soundtrack of *L'Année dernière à Marienbad* (taken from the scene preceding that of the statue), while a number of titles oblige us to reread (bit by bit) the famous phrase 'The cinema replaces our gaze with a world that accords with our desires.' As usual Godard has many images and sounds working in parallel. Extracts from famous works are juxtaposed in a magical chain that links some of the greatest names in cinema, and which, deploying a whole cluster of associations around the notions of love and desire, forms the most beautiful and exact commentary there is on *L'Année dernière à Marienbad*, with Godard's montage making appeal to what could be called 'go-between' works: the sequences chosen from *The Band Wagon* (1953) and *Faust*, the dance of seduction plus the temptation, are in thematic harmony with *L'Année dernière à Marienbad*. They also evoke each film-maker's debt to German cinema, as well as the relationship both have to musical comedy (*The Pajama Game* belongs to their respective list of favourite films). This sequence allows the subterranean dialogue between the two film-makers to finally surface, a dialogue which is the most secret and enriching aspect of French cinema since the end of the 50s.[57]

NOTES

Where, in order to avoid repetition, comments by Resnais or Robbe-Grillet have not been footnoted, the source is either *L'Arc* or the preface to *L'Année dernière à Marienbad* (see Bibliography).

1 Michel Mourlet, *La Mise en scène comme langage* (Paris: Henri Veyrier, 1987), p. 87. See, in the same book, the text entitled 'Il y a trente ans à Marienbad'.
2 Jacques Lourcelles, *Dictionnaire du Cinéma* (Paris: Robert Laffont/Bouquins, 1992), p. 1617.
3 Jacques-Bernard Brunius, 'Every Year in Marienbad or The Discipline of Uncertainty', *Sight and Sound* vol. 31 no. 3, Summer 1962, p. 123.
4 *Artsept* no. 1, January–March 1963, p. 104.
5 Geneviève Rodis-Lewis, 'Miroir de ma pensée', in *Regards sur l'art* (Paris: Beauchesne, 1993), pp. 216–17.
6 Gilles Deleuze, *Différence et répétition* (Paris: PUF, 1968), p. 376.
7 Gilles Deleuze, *L'Image-temps* (Paris: Éditions de Minuit, 1985), p. 153.
8 Claude Ollier, 'Ce soir à Marienbad', *NRF* no. 106, 1 October 1961.
9 Robert Benayoun, *Alain Resnais, arpenteur de l'imaginaire* (Paris: Ramsay Poche Cinéma, 1986 [first edition, 1980]), pp. 81–2.
10 *Des yeux pour voir*, no. 1 (Paris: Ramsay Poche Cinéma, 1971), p. 125.
11 Cited in *Premier Plan* no. 18, October 1961, p. 44.
12 Alain Robbe-Grillet, 'Temps et description dans le roman d'auhourd'hui', in *Pour un nouveau roman* (Paris: Gallimard/Idées, 1963), p. 161.
13 Benayoun, *Alain Resnais*, p. 84.
14 'Avant *L'Année dernière à Marienbad*', interview with Nicole Zand, *France-Observateur*, 18 May 1961, p. 25.
15 Jean-Daniel Roob, *Alain Resnais, qui êtes-vous?* (Lyon: La Manufacture, 1986), p. 116.
16 Ibid., p. 116.
17 *L'Arc* no. 31, 1990, p. 58.
18 Sacha Vierny in interview with Hubert Juin, 'Quatre de Marienbad', *Les Lettres françaises* no. 895, 5–11 October 1961.

19 Statement by Philippe Brun, *L'Arc* no. 31, p. 62.
20 In François Thomas, *L'Atelier d'Alain Resnais* (Paris: Flammarion, 1989), p. 115. Also see the interview with Jacques Saulnier, *Positif* nos 329–30, July–August 1988, p. 42.
21 Jacques Saulnier, p. 42.
22 Thomas, *L'Atelier*, p. 144.
23 Statement by Philippe Brun, p. 189.
24 Sacha Vierny, in Thomas, *L'Atelier*, pp. 172–3.
25 Thomas, *L'Atelier*, pp. 190–1.
26 Hubert Juin interview, 'Quatre de Marienbad'.
27 *L'Arc* no. 31, pp. 66–7.
28 Hubert Juin interview, 'Quatre de Marienbad'.
29 See the musician's statement in 'Quatre de Marienbad'.
30 An actor in both *Hiroshima mon amour* and *L'Année dernière à Marienbad*, he makes an appearance in *La Guerre est finie*.
31 Bernard Pingaut, *L'Arc* no. 31, p. 82.
32 Ibid., pp. 82–3. 'I'd asked Delphine Seyrig to avoid all tonality at particular moments in *L'Année dernière à Marienbad* (I didn't know, of course, about the restricted modes of transposition invented by Messiaen, but I was experiencing them at a physical level, and since Messiaen was our inspiration I came across these problems again)', in Thomas, *L'Atelier*, p. 260.
33 Jacques Saulnier, in Thomas, *L'Atelier*, p. 116.
34 Roob, *Alain Resnais*, p. 133.
35 Nicole Zand interview, *France-Observateur*, p. 24.
36 Benayoun, *Alain Resnais*, p. 103.
37 And doubtless due to the fact that he'd met Delphine Seyrig in New York while she was performing in another Ibsen play, *An Enemy of the People*.
38 When speaking to Resnais of the title of the play, *Rosmer*, he claimed not to have had Ibsen in mind: 'I'd thought, maybe, of Jean Rosmer, a popular novelist of the mid-20s', in *Positif* nos 329–30, p. 22.
39 Sylvette Baudrot, in Thomas, *L'Atelier*, p. 152.

40 *L'Arc* no. 31, p. 37.

41 Ibid., p. 66.

42 Jacques Saulnier, p. 43.

43 Ibid., p. 55. Like the other sets, the corridor was constructed in the Photosonor Studios 'where this was the last film but one shot before their demolition', cf. ibid., p. 42.

44 Statement by Sylvette Baudrot, in Thomas, *L'Atelier*, p. 157. See also *L'Arc* no. 31, p. 51.

45 Alain Robbe-Grillet, *L'Année dernière à Marienbad* (Paris: Éditions de Minuit, 1961), p. 28.

46 Ibid., p. 33.

47 *L'Arc* no. 31, p. 55.

48 Hubert Juin interview, 'Quatre de Marienbad'.

49 Suzanne Liandrat-Guigues, 'Des statues et des films', *Cinémathèque* no. 6, Autumn 1994, pp. 46–7. The quotation is from Claude Ollier, *Souvenirs écran* (Paris: Cahiers du Cinéma/Gallimard, 1981), p. 150.

50 Robbe-Grillet, *L'Année dernière*, p. 23.

51 One observes that the names (separate or in groups) are located below, at the top, to the right and to the left, or sometimes centred, etc. In short, they occupy every position within the frame. This wish to use the space in its entirety makes one think of what Resnais has said of Robbe-Grillet's work, which, he claims, evokes the Douanier Rousseau 'who used to begin a canvas in the top-left corner, then fill in all the details before ending up in the bottom-right corner', cf. *Cahiers du Cinéma* no. 123, p. 2. This remark also applies to Resnais, and the fanatical and meticulous side of his personality (according to witnesses).

52 Robbe-Grillet, *L'Année dernière*, p. 74.

53 Gilles Deleuze, *Différence et répétition*, pp. 374–5.

54 Jean Léon, in Thomas, *L'Atelier*, p. 144.

55 Sylvette Baudrot, in ibid., p. 148.

56 Youssef Ishaghpour, *D'une image à l'autre* (Paris: Denoël/Gonthier, 1982), p. 181. This dialogue is elucidated in part in Suzanne Liandrat-Guigues' 'Des statues et des films'.

CREDITS
....

L'Année dernière à Marienbad/L'anno scorso a Marienbad

France/Italy
1961

Production Companies
Pierre Courau and
Raymond Froment present
a French-Italian
co-production of
Terra-Film/Société
Nouvelle des Films
Cormoran/Précitel/
Como-Films/Argos-
Films/Les Films
Tamara/Cinetel/Silver-
Films (France)/Cineriz
(Rome)
Producers
Pierre Courau, Raymond
Froment
Production Manager
Léon Sanz
Unit Production Manager
Michel Choquet
Unit Manager
Jean-Jacques Lecot
Production Secretary
Janine Thaon
Director
Alain Resnais
Assistant Director
Jean Léon
2nd Assistant Directors
Volker Schlöndorff,
Florence Malraux
Script Supervisor
Sylvette Baudrot
Screenplay/Dialogues
Alain Robbe-Grillet
Director of Photography
Sacha Vierny

Camera Operator
Philippe Brun
Assistant Camera
Guy Delattre
2nd Assistant Camera
Françoise Lauliac
Key Grips
Louis Balthazard, René
Stocki
Gaffer
Elie Fontanille
Stills Photography
Georges Pierre
Editors
Henri Colpi,
Jasmine Chasney
Art Director
Jacques Saulnier
Set Decorators
Georges Glon,
André Piltant,
Jean-Jacques Fabre
Properties
Charles Mérangel
**Ms Seyrig's Two Feather
Costumes by**
Bernard Evein
**Ms Seyrig's Other
Dresses**
Chanel
Key Make-up
Alex Marcus
Make-up Artist
Eliane Marcus
Titles
Jean Fouchet F.L.
Music
Francis Seyrig
Organist
Marie Louise Girod
Music Director
André Girard
Sound
Guy Villette, Jean-Claude
Marchetti, René Renault,
Jean Nény, Robert
Cambourakis

Cast
Giorgio Albertazzi
X
Delphine Seyrig
A
Sacha Pitoëff
M
Françoise Bertin
Luce Garcia-Ville
Héléna Kornel
Françoise Spira
Karin Toeche-Mittler
Pierre Barbaud
Wilhelm von Deek
Jean Lanier
Gérard Lorin
Davide Montemuri
Gilles Quéant
Gabriel Werner

8,531 feet
94 minutes

Black-and-white
Anamorphic [Dyaliscope]

Shot at Photosonore-
Marignan-Simo Studios,
Paris and on location in
Munich and the chateaux
Nymphenburg, Schleissheim
and Amalienburg over a
period of ten weeks in
autumn 1960

Credits compiled by
Markku Salmi, BFI
Filmographic Unit

The print of *L'Année dernière
à Marienbad* in the National
Film and Television Archive
was acquired specially for the
360 Classic Feature Films
project from the French
negative (through the BFI
distribution library)

BIBLIOGRAPHY

· ·

L'Arc no. 31, 1967.

Armes, Roy, *The Cinema of Alain Resnais* (London: Zwemmer, 1968).

Artsept no. 1, January–March 1963.

Benayoun, Robert, *Alain Resnais, arpenteur de l'imaginaire* (Paris: Ramsay Poche Cinéma, 1985).

Bory, Jean-Louis, *Des yeux pour voir*, vol. 1 (Paris: Ramsay Poche Cinéma, 1971).

Brunius, Jacques-Bernard, 'Every Year in Marienbad or The Discipline of Uncertainty', *Sight and Sound* vol. 31 no. 3, Summer 1962.

Cahiers du Cinéma no. 123, September 1961.

Deleuze, Gilles, *Différence et répétition* (Paris: PUF, 1968), *Difference and Repetition*, trans. Paul Patton (New York: Columbia University Press, 1994).

——, *L'Image-temps* (Paris: Éditions de Minuit, 1985), *Cinema 2: The Time Image*, trans. Hugh Tomlinson and Robert Galeta (London: Athlone, 1989).

Ishaghpour, Youssef, *D'une image à l'autre* (Paris: Denoël/Gonthier, 1982).

Kreidl, John-Francis, *Alain Resnais* (Boston: Twayne, 1977).

Liandrat-Guigues, Susan, 'Des statues et des films', *Cinémathèque* no. 6, Autumn 1994.

Lourcelles, Jacques, *Dictionnaire du Cinéma* (Paris: Robert Laffont/Bouquins, 1992).

Monaco, James, *Alain Resnais: The Rôle of Imagination* (London: Secker and Warburg, 1976).

Mourlet, Michel, *La Mise en scène comme langage* (Paris: Henri Veyrier, 1987).

Ollier, Claude, 'Ce soir à Marienbad', *NRF* no. 106, 1 October 1961, pp. 711–19 and 906–12.

——, *Souvenirs écran* (Paris: Cahiers du Cinéma/Gallimard, 1981).

Premier Plan no. 18, 1961.

Robbe-Grillet, Alain, *L'Année dernière à Marienbad* (Paris: Éditions de Minuit, 1961).

——, *Pour un nouveau roman* (Paris: Gallimard/Idées, 1963).

Rodis-Lewis, Genenviève, *Regards sur l'art* (Paris: Beauchesne, 1993).

Roob, Jean-Daniel, *Alain Resnais, qui êtes-vous?* (Lyon: La Manufacture, 1986).

Thomas, François, *L'Atelier d'Alain Resnais* (Paris: Flammarion, 1989).

Ward, John, *Alain Resnais or, The Theme of Time* (London: Secker and Warburg/BFI, 1968).

ALSO PUBLISHED

An Actor's Revenge
Ian Breakwell

L'Âge d'or
Paul Hammond

A Matter of Life and Death
Ian Christie

Annie Hall
Peter Cowie

L'Atalante
Marina Warner

L'avventura
Geoffrey Nowell-Smith

The Big Heat
Colin McArthur

The Big Sleep
David Thomson

The Birds
Camille Paglia

Blackmail
Tom Ryall

Bonnie and Clyde
Lester D.Friedman

Boudu Saved from Drowning
Richard Boston

Bride of Frankenstein
Alberto Manguel

Brief Encounter
Richard Dyer

Das Cabinet des Dr. Caligari
David Robinson

Cat People
Kim Newman

Chinatown
Michael Eaton

Citizen Kane
Laura Mulvey

Double Indemnity
Richard Schickel

Les Enfants du paradis
Jill Forbes

42nd Street
J. Hoberman

"Fires Were Started –"
Brian Winston

The Ghost and Mrs Muir
Frieda Grafe

Greed
Jonathan Rosenbaum

Gun Crazy
Jim Kitses

High Noon
Phillip Drummond

In a Lonely Place
Dana Polan

It's a Gift
Simon Louvish

The Life and Death of Colonel Blimp
A.L. Kennedy

Lolita
Richard Corliss

M
Anton Kaes

Metropolis
Thomas Elsaesser

The Magnificent Ambersons
V.F. Perkins

Meet Me in St. Louis
Gerald Kaufman

Napoléon
Nelly Kaplan

La Nuit américaine
Roger Crittenden

Odd Man Out
Dai Vaughan

Olympia
Taylor Downing

Palm Beach Story
John Pym

Pépé le Moko
Ginette Vincendeau

Performance
Colin MacCabe

Queen Christina
Marcia Landy & Amy Villarejo

Red River
Suzanne Liandrat-Guigues

Rocco and his Brothers
Sam Rohdie

Rome Open City
David Forgacs

Sanshô Dayû
Dudley Andrew & Carole Cavanaugh

The Seventh Seal
Melvyn Bragg

Shane
Edward Countryman & Evonne von Heussen-Countryman

Singin' in the Rain
Peter Wollen

Stagecoach
Edward Buscombe

Sunrise – A Song of Two Humans
Lucy Fischer

Taxi Driver
Amy Taubin

Things to Come
Christopher Frayling

Went the Day Well?
Penelope Houston

Wild Strawberries
Philip & Kersti French

The Wizard of Oz
Salman Rushdie

If you would like further information about future BFI Film Classics or about other books on film, media and popular culture from BFI Publishing, please write to:

BFI Film Classics
BFI Publishing
21 Stephen Street
London W1P 2LN